THE
MINORITY
EXPERIENCE

Navigating Emotional
and Organizational Realities

ADRIAN PEI

IVP Books

An imprint of InterVarsity Press
Downers Grove, Illinois

InterVarsity Press
P.O. Box 1400, Downers Grove, IL 60515-1426
ivpress.com
email@ivpress.com

InterVarsity Press® is the book-publishing division of InterVarsity Christian Fellowship/USA®, a movement of students and faculty active on campus at hundreds of universities, colleges, and schools of nursing in the United States of America, and a member movement of the International Fellowship of Evangelical Students. For information about local and regional activities, visit intervarsity.org.

While any stories in this book are true, some names and identifying information may have been changed to protect the privacy of individuals.

Cover design: Faceout Studio
Interior design: Daniel van Loon

ISBN 978-0-8308-4548-4 (print)
ISBN 978-0-8308-7392-0 (digital)

Printed in the United States of America ∞

InterVarsity Press is committed to ecological stewardship and to the conservation of natural resources in all our operations. This book was printed using sustainably sourced paper.

Library of Congress Cataloging-in-Publication Data

Names: Pei, Adrian, 1978- author.
Title: The minority experience : navigating emotional and organizational
    realities / Adrian Pei.
Description: Downers Grove : InterVarsity Press, 2018. | Includes
    bibliographical references and index.
Identifiers: LCCN 2018017715 (print) | LCCN 2018025084 (ebook) | ISBN
    9780830873920 (eBook) | ISBN 9780830845484 (pbk. : alk. paper)
Subjects: LCSH: Race relations--Religious aspects--Christianity. | Ethnic
    relations--Religious aspects--Christianity. | Ethnicity--Religious
    aspects--Christianity.
Classification: LCC BT734.2 (ebook) | LCC BT734.2 .P45 2018 (print) | DDC
    248.4089--dc23
LC record available at https://lccn.loc.gov/2018017715

P	25	24	23	22	21	20	19	18	17	16	15	14	13	12	11	10	9	8	7	6	5	4	3	2
Y	37	36	35	34	33	32	31	30	29	28	27	26	25	24	23	22	21	20	19					

To my father, Jack Pei.

Your gentle conviction has shown me what a strong Asian American leader looks like. You have endured courageously through pain, sacrificed as my biggest advocate, and documented our family histories for future generations to cherish. I love you, and I am so proud to be your son.

CONTENTS

PREFACE

This was not an easy book to write.

Race is one of the most polarizing topics in the world today.[1] While some people love to read every blog and news item related to race, others don't think we should talk about it at all. Some people are eager to become more culturally intelligent, while others bemoan how they need to be so "PC" about everything.

I didn't start out trying to tackle all these issues when I started the process of this book. I just wanted to share my story—of what it was like for me growing up in the United States as a person of color and working for a majority-white organization in my adult years. However, as I read biographies of ethnic minorities and studied history books, the scope of my thinking began to broaden. I discovered certain themes. Self-doubt. Domestication. Weariness. Invisibility. There seemed to be something in common among minorities—despite disparities in time, geography, and ethnicity. These themes even appeared

in the stories of the Bible, from Moses to Daniel to Jesus himself.
I began to write these themes down.

Then as I studied current experts in racial identity formation,
I began to gain new language and categories to help me frame
my learnings, and to explain some of my own experiences as a
minority. I felt better equipped to understand and engage some
of the debates I heard around me in the office, at the dinner
table, and online. I compiled these insights as well, wondering
if they might be helpful to others too. My studies helped me to
appreciate the sobering challenge of honoring the sacred stories
of peoples who have been overlooked, while also explicating
concepts with precision and nuance. How could I do this justice?[2]

Then there was my own story. As I began to write, waves of
painful memories and nostalgia came over me. A shy, skinny
Asian American kid paralyzed in fear on the baseball field, just
trying to fit in on an all-white team. An angry teenager fuming
at racist stereotypes on the television screen. A frustrated adult
kicking furniture in his house, feeling betrayed by his minority
coworkers and friends. Those were me. Revisiting these scenes
was not easy, nor was writing about them.[3] But I resolved to face
my fears, and even decided to reach out to people from my past
to try to make peace. Some of those conversations are included
in the pages of this book.

Writing this book also happened in the midst of personal
tragedy and challenge in my family. My father suffered a massive
stroke that almost took his life. One of my daughters was diag-
nosed with special needs. Some days it was hard to muster the

energy to lift a finger to write. But in another way, this pain gave meaning to my efforts. I wanted to finish this book during the years my father still had left, to honor his sacrifices and love for me. I told him I would dedicate the book to him because of all he had taught me about life—and all the times he had encouraged me to pursue my dreams of writing. Raising my daughter was motivation enough to fight for a better world for her, as a woman and as a person of color.

So I took all of this—ethnic minority biographies, the history books, race scholars, and my own story and family circumstances—and poured it into this book. I compiled and documented all the insights and lessons I had learned, in the hope that it might help others like me.

When I write "others like me," I mean my primary audience for this book—ethnic minorities who have wrestled in any way with finding their place in society, or within a majority-white organization. I wanted to write that they might more clearly identify the emotions behind their experiences as minorities. Perhaps in the pages of overlooked history, they might uncover the events and forces that had subconsciously shaped their identity. Perhaps they might gain language and categories to name their experiences (like I did) and equip them for today's ongoing debates and conversations about race. Most of all, I wanted them to know that they were not alone.

That is why I wrote this book. Of course, I hope that others may find it useful as well. Some readers from the majority culture may be looking to understand the deeper realities of what it means to be a minority, or to gather some ideas for how to diversify their organization. Many staff from churches as well as parachurch and nonprofit organizations may have just started exploring race and diversity, and are looking to take the next step. Also, while this book is written from a faith perspective, some nonreligious readers may be interested in how Christians are seeking to address the critical issues of race and justice in our time.

Finally, I write this book from an organizational development perspective, which has been my field of study and work for over a decade. My experience leads me to believe that leading change isn't just about transforming individual behavior, but about addressing broader systemic issues. Thus, I've included research and examples from some of the leading organizational thinkers in both the ministry and corporate world, where I currently work full-time.

The primary organizational context I write about is Cru, which is the largest missions organization in the world. For about a decade, I worked for the Asian American branch of Cru, which is called Epic Movement. My experiences included leading a human resources team, developing core values, and designing ethnic minority leadership curriculum and training. My wife and I are still on staff part-time with Cru.

Some may be curious what Cru leaders think about a book like this being written about their organization. I had questions myself about whether my honest and painful experiences would be welcomed or not. However, each time I've shared my stories of challenge with white Cru leaders, they've told me how helpful they are—and to keep writing and sharing. When I pitched the idea of this book to some other Cru executives, they voiced their support and asked how they could help. As I've worked on this manuscript, I've submitted drafts to leaders in the organization for their feedback. This book is truly a work of partnership *with* Cru.

However, I've also come to see clearly that this book is not really about Cru—it's about organizations, systems, and communities where there is any gap between majority and minority cultures. As I've interviewed and talked with ethnic minority leaders in other institutions and fields, similar patterns have appeared. As I researched the history of minorities in the United States (and other countries), I found that there are common realities and challenges that have existed for centuries. So while this is my own story, and I cannot speak for other minorities, I recognize that I am walking down a path of emotional realities that countless others have walked before me—and which countless others will walk in the future. Perhaps by looking at one example, we can see some broader themes and truths and come to a deeper understanding of what it means to be a minority, in the United States and beyond.

Some readers may wonder if this book will address other groups of people beyond race—such as socioeconomic class, gender, sexuality, age, religion, physical ability, and so on. I affirm the reality of *intersectionality*, which suggests that various human aspects are interconnected, and together help us to understand issues of identity.[4] While this book focuses primarily on race, I would encourage the reader to make connections and applications as they seem appropriate.[5]

I hope that by the end of this book you will gain some new language and categories to explain your experiences. I hope you will understand the historical reasons behind peoples' emotions and reactions in the ongoing debate about race. I hope you will gain a vision for how God gives us the strength, wisdom, and resilience to endure in our work and journey. I hope you will gain practical guidance and ideas for how to take your organization to the next level in diversity. Most of all, I hope you will know that you are not alone!

INTRODUCTION

What Is a Minority?

What does it mean to be a minority? It may not be what you think or have heard.

After all, you could be fluent in Chinese language and customs, and yet not understand how Asian Americans feel like they can never truly be accepted in society. You could be the only white person in a group of a hundred people of color, and still be a "majority." You might debate for hours about immigration policy, and miss why historical events make the issue so loaded for Latinos.

That's because the minority experience isn't primarily about head knowledge—but about emotional realities of *pain*.

The minority experience isn't about sheer numbers or demographic percentages—but about who holds *power*.

The minority experience isn't just about current events and politics—but even more about how these things are impacted by *the past*.

Throughout my research on race and diversity, and my decades of work in crosscultural leadership development, I've found that these three categories define so much that is distinctive about what it means to be a minority.

Pain, power, and the past are three filters through which we can view anything related to race. When we're trying to understand what it means to be African American, do we seek to hear their emotional realities of pain? When we're seeking to diversify our organization, are we treating everyone as if they are on "equal ground," or are we understanding that some are naturally disadvantaged because of sociological disparities of power? When we talk with a coworker about a race-related topic in the news (e.g., the Dakota Access Pipeline[1]), are we asking about how the past events of history might impact the discussion? If we apply these three filters, we will be well on our way to truly understanding the minority experience.

I have structured this book in two parts. Part one is called "Understanding the Minority Experience," and chapters one, three, and four each describe a particular aspect of pain, power, and the past in depth. Chapter two provides a high-level view of these three categories and defines some terms related to race. Part two is called "Redeeming the Minority Experience." Chapter five outlines some specific applications and principles for organizations as they seek to take the next step in diversifying. Chapters six, seven, and eight provide some guidance for how minorities can use pain, power, and the past to build compassion, advocacy, and wisdom, respectively.

Throughout this book, I will define race-related terms and language as necessary, but I'd like to start with a few foundational definitions here. I've learned the importance of words, because they carry connotations of pain for some or have been used as weapons of power by others. Many words have significance from the past, and language and meaning are continually evolving.

First, there is a critical difference between the terms *ethnicity* and *race*. Confusing the two terms can be unhelpful. *Ethnicity* refers to the various ancestral attributes that distinguish a people group, including appearance, language, customs, religious practices, and so on. For instance, Irish and Italian Americans are ethnic groups.

Race, on the other hand, is a category with a history and purpose of social power. According to most scholars, race was defined as a way to unify various European ethnic groups into one—"white"—in order to establish control over those from other ethnic groups (e.g., blacks). Dr. Beverly Daniel Tatum, one of the foremost experts on racial identity, writes that "the original creation of racial categories was in the service of oppression."[2] This explains how Irish and Italian Americans used to be treated by other settlers as inferior, but at a certain point came to be seen and accepted as simply "white."[3] In *The Very Good Gospel*, activist Lisa Sharon Harper cites the example of Takao Ozawa, a Japanese man who argued before the Supreme Court in 1922 that Japanese people were white. Ozawa had been restricted from clear societal benefits that came with naturalization, so he sought to fit into a racial category that had nothing to do with his skin color or ethnic background![4]

This is such a critical distinction, because merely discussing a person's Russian or German ethnicity does not tend to lead into conversations about the shared power from which those ethnic groups have benefited by nature of being "white." That is one reason why I use the term "white" or majority culture—as a reminder of the pain, power, and past history associated with those words.

For people of color, I will use the terms that I hear most commonly used, or that people within those communities call themselves—Latino (though some use Hispanic American), Native American or Native peoples, Asian American (some differentiate between Asian Pacific Islanders and Asian Pacific Americans), South Asians, and so on. Some people of African descent prefer to use "African American," while others prefer "Black" as more inclusive of Afro-Caribbeans living in the United States. Since the sources I quote use the terms fairly interchangeably, I will do the same. When I refer to the United States I try to use "United States" instead of "America," as I recognize that many other countries are part of America (North, Central, and South). However, occasionally I use "American" to avoid literary awkwardness, or "America" for symbolic and metaphorical purposes.

From working in ethnic leadership development, I have learned that one size does not fit all; even within a minority group there are important differences. Latinos from Mexico face different realities than those from South American countries such as Peru or Argentina. Among Asian Americans, a fourth-generation Japanese American in California lives a very different life than a Hmong refugee family in Wisconsin.[5] Some discrepancies are clear as day to me—for instance, I have lived a life of far greater privilege than many poor ethnic minorities. I can never understand the suffering Native Americans, Latinos, and African Americans have endured.

While we cannot oversimplify the experiences of minorities, that doesn't mean there aren't bonds that tie us together.[6] I do want to acknowledge that many of the experiences and influences described in this book are from the Asian American community, as that is who I am.[7] However, I have sought to give examples and stories from other minority communities as well. While it is not possible to represent every minority group and subgroup, my goal is to provide examples that can apply to other contexts. My hope is that reading these stories will also catalyze other minorities to keep writing and sharing the perspectives that we need so badly to hear.

Second, let's define what we mean when we use the word *culture*. I like what professor Soong-Chan Rah writes: "Culture is a human attempt to understand the world around us. It is the programming that shapes who we are and who we are becoming. It is a social system that is shaped by the individual and that also has the capacity to shape the individual. But it is also the presence of God, the image of God, the mission of God found in the human spirit, soul, and social system."[8] In this book, I use "culture" in this broad sociological and theological sense, as in "majority culture" or "organizational culture."[9]

I've mentioned that this book is written from a perspective of faith, and some of the scholars and authors I cite are of the Christian persuasion. That isn't to say that Christians or churches have all the answers to the issue of race and diversity. In fact, many of us have been some of the worst offenders in escalating debates and taking sides along political lines. Not only that, but Christians have been complicit in some of the greatest racial abuses throughout history, including slavery.[10] As a Christian, that is part of my history, and I write as someone grieved by these corruptions and departures from what faith should be.

At the same time, I have met many Christians who advocate for justice and minority issues, and many of the authors I cite have given their work and lives for these causes. They live out what I consider "the kingdom of God"—a vision of reality that Jesus taught, where the weak and poor are uplifted, and justice and peace are pursued with courage and sacrifice (Matthew 5:1-12). In this kingdom, people love with patience and are slow to anger (1 Corinthians 13:4-8). They are not quick to judge or hurl accusations as we are used to seeing in discussions about race. As a Christian, I believe that relying on our own willpower gets us stuck in destructive cycles of debate. If we truly submit to God, there's a way to break out of these cycles. This book is written with that hope and perspective.[11]

Third, you'll notice that I intentionally use the term *minority*. Many scholars in racial studies also use the term comfortably, while a few choose not to because of the reality that people of color will soon outnumber white populations in the United States. (Both CNN and the *New York Times* report that within a generation, ethnic minorities will make up more than 50 percent of the overall population in the United States.[12])

I choose to use the term *minority* and reframe it, not in terms of demographic numbers but in terms of who holds societal power.[13] Dr. Martin Luther King Jr. once said that "equality is not only a matter of mathematics and geometry, but it's a matter of psychology. . . . It is possible to have a quantitative equality and qualitative inequality."[14] This means that many minorities are not born with the same advantages as white people, even in something as simple as expecting other people around the world to speak English rather than having to learn local dialects. This has nothing to do with numbers—consider how many people live in India and China, yet neither Hindi nor Chinese are "default" worldwide languages. Very few people I know would posit that this kind of white status and privilege will suddenly disappear during the year that ethnic minorities hit 51 percent of the United States population. Furthermore, the math just wouldn't add up. Five percent of Asian Americans together with 15 percent of Latinos does not make either group feel like 20 percent. The sum of all ethnic minorities (even above 50 percent) does not translate into one unified, dominant force.

Finally, for some people, the words *emotions* and *emotional* can have connotations that aren't positive—such as lacking stability, composure, or resilience. When I use these words, I mean the deeper forces that drive human beings, such as needs, desires, and fears. I believe that while many of us like to think we are mostly rational beings, emotions drive the vast majority of our decisions and actions. So that is why I choose to focus on uncovering some of the deepest emotional realities for minorities in the chapters that follow.

As you read, pay attention to what kinds of emotions and reactions are brought to the surface. Which stories make you sad or stir up your sense of injustice? Which experiences remind you of your own childhood or past? What questions do you have, and what do you still want to learn more about? I've included some reflection and discussion questions at the end of the book, so that you can have a conversation with a friend, coworker, or small group as you read.

There's so much to learn—and every lesson reminds me that we all can make a difference in the ongoing conversation about race, power, and diversity. There may be no better time for this discussion, as racial tension and violence persists in the news and crosscultural conversations appear as polarizing as ever. We all have a story to share, and we all have an important role to play in this conversation.

PART 1

UNDERSTANDING THE MINORITY EXPERIENCE

SELF-DOUBT

Understanding Pain

Am I the problem?

I saw the world spinning around me. Our tiny rental car was thrown across four lanes of the highway, struck by an oversized truck at 70 miles per hour. My wife, Jenny, clutched my arm and gasped with desperation, "What is happening to us, Adrian?"

I felt utterly helpless, as my steering and brakes no longer had any effect. I couldn't do anything to control or slow our car's trajectory—I could only watch as we passed right in front of oncoming cars and finally smashed into a concrete divider.

It felt like the world slowed down as I looked over to see that Jenny was still there and intact. I then inspected my arms and legs, not knowing if I had broken or lost a limb—I couldn't feel anything because of the shock and adrenaline. As we slowly crawled out of our rental and saw that it was completely totaled, it was hard to believe that we were physically unharmed.

With the help of some friendly people who stopped, we filed a police report and got our car towed. The truck that struck us never stopped; it was a hit-and-run accident. But I realized then that during the previous few weeks, we had been side-swiped by an even more powerful force—cultural and organizational shock. It turned out to be the breaking point for us.

THREE BOTTLES OF SOY SAUCE

Three weeks before our accident, Jenny and I picked up that rental car at the Orlando airport and navigated our way to a small town called Winter Park, where we were to go through Cru's six-week training for new employees.

We arrived at our Rollins College apartment at night, where we picked up some boxes we had shipped out ahead of time. I had to laugh at myself as I unpackaged the three bottles of soy sauce I had packed. It's not as if there were no grocery stores selling Asian ingredients in Florida, but I guess it gave me comfort to know I could bring something familiar to a new place.

In some ways, my instincts were right. Jenny and I were only among a handful of ethnic minority staff at the training, and most of our peers were white and straight out of college.

The first few days of training were well-organized and packed with activities. Most days, we would get up around 6:30 a.m. to prepare for the day, since I was a teacher's aide for one of the training classes. We would then hear from speakers, including the president of Cru, Steve Douglass. In the afternoons, Jenny and I attended smaller breakout groups ("sections") for deeper discussion about topics such as theology. These sections were mostly organized by geographical region, so most of the time we were the only ethnic minorities in the room. However, everyone treated us nicely, and we were doing fine—until we hit our first roadblock.

SHOULD I SAY SOMETHING?

"Be careful of heresy," our section leader Richard warned as he passed around a stapled packet containing quotes from various philosophies and religious sects that diverged from the Christian faith. He walked our class through why they were false or misleading.

I don't think his intentions were bad. When I became a Christian and entered college, I majored in religious studies so I could understand the differences between various philosophies and religions from history.

But as Richard went through his packet, and soon my classmates began talking about why these divergent views were dangerous, I felt a bit defensive. I was a Christian like him and everyone else in the classroom, and yet there was something about this approach that bothered me. Maybe it felt a bit like "us and them," and maybe I couldn't help but notice that I was different from everyone in my section.

After all, when the young woman next to me gave her critique about Islam and Buddhism, those were part of the Asian traditions that shaped my grandparents and parents. They weren't just abstract concepts that I could mark up with a red pen, but were intimately intertwined with my family and cultural history—regardless of whether I agreed with them or not. Nobody else in the classroom could understand this the way Jenny and I did.

A thousand thoughts and reactions went through my head. *Should I say something? But maybe they'll think I'm trying to cause controversy. We've just started this class, so why stir the pot? Maybe Richard will clarify what he really means, and add more context later.*

I froze and didn't say a word.

But Jenny raised her hand. "If we're learning to read the Bible in context in this class, isn't it fair to also look at these passages in their context? We may not agree with them, but these traditions have history, and are sacred to many people."

I looked over at her with gratitude, and then back at the classroom and Richard.

He looked directly at Jenny, and I couldn't tell if he was angry or passionate, but he spoke with great emotion. I recall him using the words *heretics* and *eternal judgment*, but what I remember most was the look on Jenny's face as she heard the response to her question. She was stunned and confused, but mostly it felt as if she had been silenced—by Richard, and by our classmates' lack of response.

I couldn't hear a single word in the class after that.

I tried to wrap my mind around what had just happened. Did Richard understand my wife's question? Did others in the classroom feel the same way about the packet, or were we the only ones?

At dinner that day, I pulled aside a classmate and asked him what he thought about what had happened. He told me he didn't really remember much.

I was starting to second-guess myself like never before.

NUMB

A couple of days later, we did a training exercise for a different class. We were supposed to initiate conversations about spirituality with people in the local community, or people that we knew. It wasn't an easy thing to do, but Jenny and I had a few deep, respectful, and encouraging conversations through this exercise.

However, I'll never forget the evening when I got a knock on my door from one of my classmates, Cindy.

"Do you have a few minutes to talk, Adrian?" she asked.

"Of course. Is everything okay?" I replied. Cindy lived in the same apartment building as us, and she looked clearly distraught.

"Well, not really. I was out talking to people in the community today, and there was a man who had just talked to someone else from our group of trainees. He told me that person had told him in a disrespectful tone that he was going to hell."

"Wow, really?"

"Yeah. And this didn't seem right to me. Anyway, I know you're a teacher's aide, so do you think we should talk to the teacher about this? Maybe he can make a comment to the class about things like this."

"Um . . . absolutely. I think that's a great idea. I'll mention it to him tomorrow morning. Thank you so much for telling me about this." I was genuinely touched by her sensitivity and desire to respect others, which I sensed in the vast majority of my fellow trainees. Although it was hard to hear about her experience, I saw something good here. And it gave me hope.

The next morning, after I had finished my photocopy job for the upcoming lecture, I went up to the teacher sitting in his chair near the podium and explained my conversation with Cindy and what she had experienced.

"Do you think you could possibly say something to the class?" I asked.

He thought for a minute, looked down at his notes, and then gave me a dry smile. "I don't know if there is anything we can do about that."

I was so surprised that I couldn't even think of a reply. I sat down in my chair and listened to the lecture, and wondered what Cindy might be thinking.

I realized for the first time that I was starting to feel numb.

WOULD IT BE EASIER TO DISAPPEAR?

These experiences add up. By the end of our third week of training, I realized that our attempts to voice our convictions and values were going nowhere. There was no malicious intent or behavior—only silence or resistance when we tried to suggest any differences of opinion or changes. After a while, I had to wonder, does it really matter whether we say something or not? Will it make any difference? And if not, is this really a place where I can be myself and bring what I have to offer to the table?

I tried to reach out and build better relationships with Richard and our fellow trainees, but nothing seemed to stick. I felt awkward at social gatherings, and found myself hesitating when Richard or my classmates made comments I disagreed with. I had thought I knew how to handle these kinds of situations, but instead I found myself disengaging and withdrawing.

There was something new happening inside me that I didn't yet understand.

This all brought me to my breaking point one evening as my wife collapsed on our apartment couch with exhaustion. She hadn't been eating much food at meals, as her spirits were so low. I wondered if it might be a healthy decision for us to consider leaving the training early. In desperation, I reached out to some friends for counsel. They were very supportive, but some of them encouraged me to not quit and "finish what we started."

I was torn up inside, and didn't know what to do. I remember yelling in frustration. I had never doubted myself so much in my life.

So I took out my laptop computer and started to vent my raw emotions. I needed to try to make some sense of what was happening to me. Here's an excerpt from what I wrote:

> Thoughts race through my head: "Stop being so negative. Why is that Asian couple never around at these events?"
>
> The way others look at you, it begins to wear on you. Your thoughts turn into endless speculations. Your frustration turns into imaginary arguments and justifications

within your own head. The battles with insecurity, the strange feeling of isolation. If it all became bottled up inside a person, with no outlet or supportive community, it's easy to visualize the steps along the path to depression.

And so here we are, at the end of week 3, feeling physically drained and emotionally discouraged. For three weeks, we have tried to simply to be who we are, and we have found that we sadly are not able to. Our honesty is met with silence, our perspectives quenched by defensiveness; our contributions do not seem to be appreciated by our peers, nor honored by our leaders. . . . They seem to just disappear like tiny, disconnected dots on a large canvas.

When we were absent from class for two days last week, I actually wondered, "Will it be less awkward for others, now that we're not around? Would it just be easier for us to disappear? Would it really make a difference?"

That night was one of the longest of my life. In the morning, however, Jenny and I did come up with an idea. It was the weekend and we had a free day, so why not take a short break and go to Disney World? It might help to get some space from everything we were experiencing, and then we could re-evaluate things with fresh eyes afterwards. So we headed off for the day, ready for some relaxation and fun.

That was the day of our car accident.

When we returned to our apartment that evening, we told some of our peers about what had happened. They were sympathetic, but there wasn't much anybody did to follow up, let alone ask us about how we were doing emotionally after such a traumatic experience. We actually felt more support from our taxi driver from Haiti, who offered to pray for us as he drove us back to our apartment. That night, we wanted to leave the training—not just because we were in pain, but *because we felt that nobody could truly see our pain.*

A couple of days later, I set up a meeting with the director of the employee training. I shared with her our experiences and why we were considering leaving. She was gracious and kind, but still encouraged us to continue with the training. When I insisted that there were cultural realities that were impacting us significantly, she finally relented.

I wish I could have explained to the training director the emotional realities I was facing as a minority, or the organizational forces Jenny and I were trying to navigate. But I didn't fully understand them at the time. What did strike me was that it took us telling people that we were thinking of leaving in order to draw attention to the fact that something was wrong or needed to be addressed.

Again, we weren't facing malicious behavior, but rather something much more subtle—a culture of power that resisted differences, and a culture of passivity in response to pain. In such an environment, the unspoken message was, "We won't think about you, unless we're forced to." Not unlike our car accident, we felt helpless to stop these forces that had sideswiped and spun us around. This was another hit-and-run that we didn't see coming, and it struck me even more deeply because it made me question my very identity.

DECONSTRUCTION

Now that I've had time to reflect on our training experience, I can see that Jenny and I experienced a key component of the minority experience—self-doubt. This self-doubt comes from repeated experiences of being different, being questioned or regarded with suspicion, and even being silenced and shut down. Self-doubt comes from experiences of pain.

When Richard was deconstructing that booklet of divergent beliefs in our section, he was deconstructing a piece of us. When our classmates were talking about "us" and "them," part of us felt like "them." We felt like the "other."

It hurt. I felt naked and exposed in front of the rest of the class.

After all, feeling like I'm on the outside—that's part of my experience as a minority. Every time someone asks me "what country I come from" or remarks on how well I speak English, it's a reminder that maybe I don't quite belong. As much as I want and try to fit in, I have this sinking feeling that it won't ever be enough, and I'll always be on the outside looking in.

I feel alone. Maybe I shouldn't be here. Maybe I am the "other."

It strikes me that we didn't start off the training in any great and obvious pain, or with a chip on our shoulders. We came in confident, equipped, and prepared in many ways. So when I started to second-guess my instincts and decisions at every turn, it took me by surprise. My feelings of anger, insecurity, paranoia, and even depression—I didn't expect them, nor did I know what to do with them.

I started to wonder, "Am I not seeing things clearly? Am I the only one who thinks this way? Or maybe, am *I* the problem?"

INTERNALIZING THE BLAME

In the past decade, Western societies have become increasingly aware of the realities of shame, especially due to the work of *Daring Greatly* author Brené Brown and HonorShame.com blogger Jayson Georges. I still remember a 2006 report by CNN on the high rates of suicide among Asian American women between the ages of fifteen and twenty-four and the way this article circulated through minority communities.[1] Taboo topics like suicide, mental health, depression, and shame were finally getting more widespread attention.

Unfortunately, the reports of suicide keep coming in. *Washington Post* columnist Jeff Yang wrote about a string of four suicides in a span of six months at Palo Alto's Gunn High School.[2] Three of the four students who took their lives were Asian American. Yang writes of the exceedingly high pressure for these kids to succeed academically.

I know this very well myself, as I worked for years as a high school counselor to hundreds of Asian American students, including many from Gunn. I still recall stories of parents telling me to give their children more work to do, even when the teenagers barely had time to sleep or socialize. I remember the students who had hit their breaking point and came to me in tears.

When these Asian American students could no longer handle the pressure, they didn't fight back, but instead internalized the pressure and blame on themselves. It was shame and self-blame. The impact of their painful experiences was to conclude that *they* were the problem. And tragically, when kids have no safe outlet for talking about these things in their own families, sometimes they feel the only way out is to take their own lives. Cindy Ng, the associate dean of students and director of the Asian American Activities Center at Stanford University, describes how failures become internalized for minorities, leading to "feelings of failure and worthlessness."[3]

Brené Brown makes a clear distinction between shame and guilt. She defines guilt as "holding something we've done or failed to do up against our values and feeling psychological discomfort." This, Brown believes, can be helpful in a way that shame is not. She defines shame as "the intensely painful feeling or experience of believing that we are flawed and therefore unworthy of love and belonging."[4]

Andy Crouch published an article in *Christianity Today* about the dynamics of shame that Western societies are beginning to uncover—especially in contexts such as social media "communities." He writes of a culture where "people yearn to feel included in the group, a state constantly endangered, fragile, and desperately in need of protection."[5] *New York Times* opinion writer David Brooks agrees with Crouch, writing that our modern shame culture can be "strangely unmerciful to those who disagree and to those who don't fit in."[6]

As I think of our experiences at Cru's new staff training, so much of this language of shame resonates. Jenny and I were the ones who disagreed and chose to speak our minds to our section leader, teacher, and other people in leadership. Despite our efforts, we felt all the ways we didn't fit in as minorities. And as we discovered that "being ourselves" resulted in defensiveness and silencing, we started to *internalize* the failure and blame. We didn't just feel guilt as Brown defines it; we began to question whether we were worthy of love and belonging in this group. We began to wonder if we were the ones who were the problem. I didn't think of taking my own life, but I did wonder if it would just be better if I "went away." I was starting to grasp the minority experience of *pain*.

This was a shock to my system, because I had always thought of myself as a confident, socially adjusted person who had assimilated into North American culture. Why was I feeling like this?

NO VACANCY

As I later discovered, my feelings of self-doubt and shame didn't just come from inside my head, but from centuries of negative messages in North American society towards ethnic minorities. Daniel Sanchez describes how the majority culture's stereotypes of Latinos are perpetuated in "educational systems, commercial advertising, and mass media reporting" and contribute to the formation of a negative Latino self-image. He quotes Virgilio Elizondo, who summarizes the process of internalizing blame: "If you hear again and again that you are inferior, good for nothing, incompetent, and lazy, you may eventually begin to believe it yourself."[7]

In *The Warmth of Other Suns*, Pulitzer Prize–winning author Isabel Wilkerson tells the true story of Robert Joseph Pershing Foster, an African American man looking for a motel room as he drove through Phoenix, Arizona, in 1953. This powerful account illustrates the self-doubt of the minority experience.

Time after time, Foster is turned away from motels—some with a blatant "Vacancy" lighted sign. Although it is clear that he is not welcome because he is black, Foster begins to replay the rejections in his mind and doubt his own approach. He wonders if he hadn't explained himself well enough, and so he rehearses his speech to the next motel receptionist over and over, "debating with himself as to what he should say."[8]

Finally, in his exhaustion, Foster decides to confront a motel owner couple, and asks them to simply tell him if they don't allow blacks to stay over. The husband and wife tell him that they actually don't agree with segregation practices, but if they were to take Foster in, they would be ostracized by the other motel owners and risk losing their business.

Foster moves on, and later that night describes his plight to a friendly gas station owner. While the owner tries to console him, Foster reflects on his minority experience: he has experienced so much dehumanization that he begins to doubt his own worth and actions. When it becomes clear that he isn't out of his mind, it doesn't make things any easier to bear. After all, there is a systemic injustice here that the motel and gas station owners know is wrong, but Foster is still without a motel room, and "nobody of a mind to do anything had done a single thing to change that fact." Foster concludes, "That made the pain harder, not easier, to bear."[9] Foster's self-doubt wasn't just in his own head, but came from painful *realities* of discrimination. When we understand history, this becomes clearer.[10]

MOSES' MINORITY TRAUMA

Another example of self-doubt and pain comes straight from the pages of the Bible in the leadership journey of Moses. It is well known that Moses doubted himself—citing numerous reasons why he should not be the person to lead the Israelites— even when confronted by the presence and commands of God (Exodus 3:1–4:17). What kinds of painful realities from Moses' experiences as a minority might have caused him to have such intense feelings of unworthiness?

Consider that Moses was born in the midst of minority persecution, as all Israelite male babies were ordered by the king of Egypt to be killed or thrown into the Nile River (Exodus 1:15-22). Moses was one of those babies put into the river, so one of his first experiences was abandonment (Exodus 2:1-4). Then he was raised within Egyptian culture—the very people who had killed his own people and now enslaved them. He may not have even discovered his true ethnic identity until he was an adult, which would have not only been confusing but traumatic.[11] Perhaps this explains his reaction of killing the Egyptian who was beating an Israelite in the desert (Exodus 2:11-12).

After seeing mostly negative, powerless images of the enslaved Israelites, it is not hard to imagine how Moses might have questioned his own worth and doubted himself. In response, God did not tell Moses to "step up" or "get over his past," but provided him with a team so he didn't have to do things alone. God told Moses to work with his brother Aaron and use their different strengths to complement one another (Exodus 4:14-16). Moses, Aaron, and their sister, Miriam, form a team that helps to lead the people of Israel (Exodus 15; Numbers 12). Later, Moses took the advice of his father-in-law, Jethro, to delegate his governing responsibilities among a variety of leaders, so all the pressure wouldn't be on Moses (Exodus 18:13-27). Throughout Moses' life, you can see how he slowly grows to accept his responsibilities and gains confidence in his ability to lead (Exodus 33:12-23).

Moses is an intriguing example of a leader that God challenges, but also gives space to heal and grow into leadership—especially through the help of partners and wise advisors. In my experience working with ethnic minority leaders, many tend to doubt themselves because they are starting with so many negative messages and painful experiences from their past. Recognizing the root cause of this self-doubt can help us to be patient and supportive in their leadership journey.

TEN YEARS LATER: A CONVERSATION WITH RICHARD

As for me, self-doubt turned out to be a gift from God. Because I was forced to question myself on such a deep level, I gained greater clarity about why I felt those emotions and what to do about them.

For one, Jenny and I decided to leave our new staff training so we could heal and regroup. We met up with minority leaders from Epic Movement to debrief our experiences. It was in those next few critical months that we gained even greater motivation to continue our work with Cru and Epic. I thought to myself, "Now I understand much more clearly what minorities experience, and how I can serve and support them." So Jenny and I returned to Florida a few months later to finish up our training, but we were far more equipped and purposeful.

Also, about a decade later I decided to reach out to Richard. Now that I had more clarity, I wanted to share our experiences in his section and to hear his recollections and perspective. I had chosen before to disengage and withdraw from these painful experiences, but I wanted to face them. So I reached out to Richard to see if he had time to talk.

I'll admit that it was very hard to do this. After all, it had been such a long time since our training, and I didn't even know if Richard remembered who I was! Also, wouldn't it just be easier to let bygones be bygones? However, I realized that Richard might not even know that there were bygones at all, because I had never directly told him about our painful experiences in his section.

Fortunately, Richard did remember me, and graciously accepted to take a call. After catching up a bit, I shared about the booklet about "divergent perspectives" and its impact on me and Jenny. At first, Richard felt bad and said that he would never have given out the booklet if he knew what it would do to us. Then, he questioned whether or not the contents of the booklet were what we remembered them to be. I felt myself starting to drift into self-doubt territory, but then corrected myself and said, "Whatever the booklet said, my experience in the class and training made me feel like I was different from everyone else."

My sense was that Richard was struggling to move on from talking about what was in the booklet, and he felt some responsibility and even guilt about the painful experience that Jenny and I had. I felt torn because part of me felt uncomfortable letting him feel my pain. I wanted to own what I could have done differently—for instance, I could have had a direct conversation with him about what was bothering me.

Later in the conversation, Richard asked me, "What was the training like for you as an ethnic minority? Did you feel supported by your peers and able to approach me with your concerns?"

I shared my feelings of self-doubt, insecurity, and paranoia—and how those emotions took me by surprise. I shared that I found it harder than I thought to approach or confront him, because he was white and had a strong, confident personality. I told him that I might have been afraid that if I did voice my emotions, he or other Cru leaders might not accept me.

Richard responded by acknowledging that it was his job to make sure we felt safe in that environment, but that he was also new to his role and didn't fully understand how to do that for us. He told me how he's learned a lot in the past decade, and has become more aware of the need to discuss cultural issues, and understand minorities' realities. Moreover, he told me of some efforts Cru has made in recent years to improve cultural sensitivity during their new staff training and theological classes. For instance, key assignments for trainees now include studying historical-cultural issues like slavery, and discussion questions acknowledge racial power and ethnic superiority, including the Jewish-Gentile divide.[12]

Richard and I had a productive conversation, and I told him about my plan to write a book including my experiences at new staff training. A few months later, Richard reached out to me to ask to talk again, as he had remembered another detail that he thought might have impacted our experience at training—a blunt comment he had written on one of our papers. I didn't even remember this comment, but it touched me that Richard was thinking about what our reality has been as minorities. I walked away from our dialogues with a sense of confirmation that it's never too late to face unresolved issues from our past, as hard as it was to initiate and navigate these conversations.

Many conversations and relationships such as this are messy, and they don't often go as we might want or hope. However, I didn't do it to change Richard, but as a step of personal growth to face my unresolved issues and past. As I've taken steps like this, it's only clarified my sense of purpose in work and life—and shown me where I still need to learn and grow.

Indeed, through all my experiences at Cru's new staff training, I sensed I was only scratching the surface of the minority experience, and I wanted to learn more about African American,

Latino, and Native American history with fresh eyes. I thought I was well adjusted to living in the United States, but I learned how much had been suppressed and buried under the surface.

My journey in understanding the minority experience had just begun.

PAIN, POWER, AND THE PAST

Three Distinctives of the Minority Experience

Since our new staff training experience, I've had a number of conversations with Cru leaders who have thoughts about how to make the training a better experience for minorities. And there is a lot of interest and energy organizationally (and in the United States) to change things and "fix" the diversity issue.

However, in my organizational development work in both corporate and ministry settings, I frequently see diversity treated as a depersonalized strategy or tactic. Leaders identify a benchmark for how many ethnic minority leaders they want to fill "X" positions, or they just want to see some improvement in demographic numbers from the previous year. These approaches fall short of truly improving the organization, because they don't connect with the meaning of *why* diversity is important. Do we value diversity simply because we feel like it's the politically correct thing to do, or so that our organization looks better?

Do we pursue diversity simply because our president or CEO told us we need to focus on it?

Ultimately, diversity is about the value and dignity of people—ethnic minorities—whose unique voices have been overlooked or even silenced. It is about restoring beautiful missing pieces of the canvas of history that can enrich our view of the world, and of God. It is about acknowledging pains and injustices of power from the past.

It may feel a bit heavy to address those topics, which may be why so many organizations find it easier to stay at "safe" and superficial "tactical" levels that don't require as much from them.

For instance, we might focus on implementing a cultural competency training class for our organization. Frequently, these programs focus on giving people tools to navigate differences in language, customs, values, time perception, and many other categories. While there is value in this, competency training programs frequently fall short of acknowledging issues of justice and power—which are the heartbeat behind why diversity matters, and what drives nearly every current debate about race. These trainings tend to focus on ethnicity rather than on race. They put the onus of cultural growth equally on everyone rather than acknowledging existing structures that favor the majority culture.

Or we might look only skin-deep in filling leadership roles. If a person has an ethnic minority "sounding" name or appearance, we may be content to simply check the box of diversity—regardless of his or her ability to represent the uniqueness of their culture in the workplace. When I talked to Dr. Daniel Lee, director of Fuller Theological Seminary's Asian American Studies Center,[1] he described this practice as "cosmetic diversity."[2] He told me that this approach backfires because the minority leaders who rise up the ranks are often those who have learned to "act more white" in order to fit in with the dominant culture. So in the end, we're not diversifying our organizations as much as we think we are.

When we approach diversity in this pragmatic way, we make the mistake of treating minorities as a means to an end. They help us achieve our goals and visions instead of shaping the vision and process themselves.

But when we treat minorities as having inherent value, we will take a different approach. We will seek to listen and learn about how we can better serve and represent minorities and their deepest needs. We will ask them, "What perspectives and contributions are we missing?" We will give minorities authority to shape and influence the diversification process. And we will look deeper than cosmetic diversity into realities of pain, power, and the past.

To transform our organizations, we must understand the minority experience.

PAIN, POWER, AND THE PAST

These three *categories* can help us differentiate the minority experience—pain, power, and the past.

When I think about my new staff training experience, I experienced something that couldn't be fixed by mere cultural knowledge. For instance, if one of my white coworkers had known more about Asian American traditions or values (e.g., "Asian Americans can be more indirect in their communication style"), I doubt it would have helped them address the emotional realities of my self-doubt, paranoia, and depression.

It certainly would *not* have helped if someone had told me during the training, "Hey, I get it. I'm white and I have an ethnicity too. You're trying to be yourself, and I'm trying to be myself. We're just different and have to listen to and respect each other."

No . . . I experienced a very *real* difference from my majority culture peers that I couldn't deny or minimize. They didn't have to think about and worry about the same things I did. I had a burden they didn't, and they experienced a comfort I didn't and couldn't experience.

What was this all about?

It wasn't primarily about ethnicity. It was about the realities and dynamics of what it means to be a minority amidst the majority culture.

It was a difference in the *pain* that surfaced from the unique doubts, challenges, and struggles I faced as a minority.

It was a difference in our place in this country, as majority and minorities. It was a difference in *power*.

It was a difference in our *past*. It tapped into something deep that was inside me, but was also far deeper and beyond me. My history wasn't just about me, but about my family and the previous generations of my ethnic heritage.

PAIN

"You weren't born by the river!"

My wife shouted at our television screen indignantly as we watched the auditions for *American Idol*. The contestant, a young white male in khakis, had just delivered an over-the-top rendition of Sam Cooke's "A Change Is Gonna Come," a song about racial injustice that begins with the line "I was born by the river, in a little tent . . ."

I had to chuckle. I admired the sincerity of the contestant, who probably loved the song and wanted to perform it well in front of judge Simon Cowell's glaring gaze. But beyond this young man's sincerity and behind our amusement, there was a real disconnect that my wife and I were feeling. Here are some of the lyrics to the song:

> I go to the movie and I go downtown
> Somebody keep telling me don't hang around[3]

"A Change Is Gonna Come" describes the painful realities of segregation, discrimination, and racially motivated violence for African Americans. This song resonated powerfully with their community and became a kind of anthem of the Civil Rights Movement of the 1960s because it captured a pain that was unique to African Americans' history as minorities in the United States. It was inspired by a harrowing experience that singer Sam Cooke had at a motel when he was denied a room because he was African American. As he protested, Cooke's wife pleaded with him to stop, saying, "They'll kill you."[4] Although he did

eventually relent, Cooke was later tragically shot and killed at a
motel in Los Angeles—only two weeks before "A Change Is
Gonna Come" was released.

There's a history of minority pain in this song. How could this
wealthy, suburban white man on *American Idol* understand the
realities of having to flee and run constantly out of fear of racial
persecution? How could he understand segregation and being
denied at the movies, as the song describes? How could he understand the weariness of longing for change and justice but
getting knocked down every time he began to hope, as the
song describes?

That doesn't mean the young white man hadn't had his fair
share of struggles and challenges. For all we knew, he could have
grown up in poverty, or experienced abuse in his household. This
man might have been bullied and made fun of constantly by his
peers. Maybe he even battled depression and suicide. I'm not
trying to minimize the very serious and real challenges of those
in the majority culture. I'm not trying to compare or judge levels
of pain that people have endured in their lives.

What I'm trying to do is clarify that minorities experience a
unique and *additional* layer of pain that those from the majority
culture simply do not have to deal with. It's the pain that comes
from minority injustices, from slavery and Japanese internment
camps to racial slurs and negative stereotypes in the media. It's
the pain that comes from not knowing if you belong in this
country simply because of your race. It's the pain that comes

from unequal treatment and fewer opportunities due to one's race. These are all realities of the minority experience.

It's so important to make this distinction, because if there's one thing I've learned in my crosscultural experiences working with thousands of people—*there is an irresistible temptation to simplify things by placing everyone in the "same" category.* Every time I discuss the pain of minorities, someone in the room tends to mention that "white people experience pain too." Every time I discuss stories or culture of minorities, someone in the room will remind me that white people have stories and a culture too. If you haven't seen or experienced this kind of reaction yourself yet, I guarantee you will in the near future.

There's always an attempt to equalize people and experiences, and it's almost always done in reaction to attempts by minorities to assert their own distinctiveness or value. Consider the Black Lives Matter movement, which arose out of a Facebook conversation between two ethnic minority women, Patrisse Cullors and Alicia Garza, after the acquittal of George Zimmerman in the shooting death of African American teen Trayvon Martin. Black Lives Matter originated as a cry for justice and humanity amidst a long history of injustice and inhumanity experienced by African Americans. Dr. Leah Gunning Francis writes in *Ferguson & Faith* that to say that Black Lives Matter is to

(1) see black people as human beings and not racist stereotypes; (2) affirm the human dignity and value of black people as equal to all other people; and (3) challenge the

hearer or reader to consider what it means to create a social order that values the lives of black people in all facets of their existence.[5]

The context of the movement clearly defines a need to assert the value of black dignity and worth due to a lack of such value throughout history. But what has been the reaction to this movement from some in the majority culture? The phrase "All Lives Matter."

On the surface, this statement may not seem problematic. But if white people really lived out All Lives Matter, it would actually raise the bar on their commitment to do more on behalf of blacks, Latinos, Asian Americans, Native Americans, refugees, and so on. Unfortunately, we rarely see such action follow such a statement. Instead, reactionary statements like this tend to shut down conversations. They tend to discourage the expressiveness of minorities, who are often trying to define who they are or bring attention to the pain they have experienced.

Put another way: I don't hear people saying, *Yes, keep saying "Black Lives Matter." And we need more movements like it.*

Instead I hear, *Why have a Black Lives Matter movement? It's divisive and controversial. Let's not focus on any racial group like that.*

Do you see the difference in these two approaches? The first approach encourages further minority expression, while the second approach discourages it. The first leads to more action, while the second evades responsibility.

Moreover, there is an even bigger problem with the "equalizing" response, especially when whites interject "White Lives Matter, too." Simply put, ethnic minorities and whites are not on equal ground. To claim that white pain is the same as black pain is not only unhelpful—it's simply not accurate.

Activist and professor Drew Hart illustrates this well in his book *Trouble I've Seen*. He tells the story of meeting up for sweet tea with a friendly white suburban pastor, who placed his foam cup on the table between them and decided to make a racial analogy. The white pastor said, "Because I can't see what is on your side of the cup, I need you to share with me your perspective so I can see things from your standpoint. Likewise, you need me to share my point of view so that you can understand the world from my vantage point."

Hart reflects that while this was a nice sentiment, it was a naive assumption that the two men were on equal ground.[6] Hart graciously but firmly corrected his pastor friend, explaining that Hart had learned Eurocentric history, read white literature and lectures, studied under mostly white teachers, and lived for many years in white communities. On the other hand, the white pastor could easily have gone his entire life without needing to know black literature, art, music, and history. He could choose to never engage with the black community, and he would never be penalized in his livelihood or economic status for that.[7]

Hart exposes the oversimplified image that many people have in the mind when it comes to race relations—two people of different *ethnicities* sit down and share stories across a table. This structure ignores the vast gaps in pain, power, and the past between whites and ethnic minorities. Instead of a horizontal divide between two people on equal standing, Hart encourages readers to picture a vertically structured hierarchy based on the power gap between *races*.[8]

Now, there is no question that people from the majority culture experience pain. But what kind of pain? And from where does the pain originate? If we're honest, the answers to those questions lead us down vastly different paths from ethnic minorities. There is simply no way that whites in North America can understand the pain of Native Americans who had their homeland invaded and taken away, because that is not part of their experience. Native Americans experience a very specific layer of pain that we cannot (and should not) try to equalize.

These days it seems popular in crosscultural settings to say that we need to "listen to each other's stories." This is a great starting point, but we need to go one step further. We need to start talking about and listening to *stories of minority pain*.

Here's an example, straight from the life story of an African American leader in Cru, Charles Gilmer. In his book *A Cry of Hope, a Call to Action*, Gilmer shares,

> I learned that when we traveled south from our home in
> West Virginia, we could not assume that restroom facilities
> at gas stations and other public accommodations were at
> our disposal. I learned that our White neighbors across the
> road that ran up the little hollow in which we lived did not

want us to play with their grandchildren. I learned that you did not want to be out in certain parts of the county after dark. Just driving your car through the neighborhood could get you in trouble—just because you were Black.[9]

How have minorities been impacted by negative stereotypes of their race in the media? When have minorities felt excluded or discriminated against because of race? These are just a couple of examples of conversations that need to happen more often.

We need to go deeper than just talking about ethnic customs and values—and address minority pain.

POWER

There is a phrase in the Japanese language, *shikata ga nai*, that is translated as "It cannot be helped." In Jeanne Wakatsuki Houston's book *Farewell to Manzanar*, an entire chapter explores this phrase and sentiment that captures the apparent passivity of the Japanese in the face of oppression during World War II, when many Japanese American residents of the United States were put into internment camps.

One of the saddest aspects of Houston's book is her description of how her father was "broken down" in the internment camps. Almost overnight, he went from being a proud and contributing American to being an object of fear and scorn. Houston writes about her father,

But I think he knew it was futile to hide out or resist. . . . He didn't struggle. There was no point to it. He had become a man without a country. The land of his birth was at war with America; yet after thirty-five years here he was still prevented by law from becoming an American citizen. He was suddenly a man with no rights who looked exactly like the enemy.[10]

Simply put, this description of the minority experience has to do with power—the powerlessness that a group of people experiences as they are forced against their will into horrific circumstances.

It's not about whether or not they tried to assert themselves. Some Japanese Americans did fight back or tried to escape the internment camps, but were shot. On a global scale, the Japanese who fought during World War II were ultimately shut down by the ultimate display of power—the atomic bomb. Not once but twice this weapon effectively silenced the Japanese people, and this had an impact that carries to this day in the country's memory.

When Emperor Hirohito was asked about the bombings in 1975, he responded, "It's very regrettable that nuclear bombs were dropped and I feel sorry for the citizens of Hiroshima, but it couldn't be helped [*shikata ga nai*] because that happened in wartime."[11]

Shikata ga nai captures an aspect of the minority experience that whites in the United States cannot relate to. This doesn't mean that whites haven't experienced helplessness or despair. However, they do not share the historical realities of minorities such as the Native Choctaw and Cherokee tribes, who tried to resist the western advance of white settlers, but were manipulated into giving up their land.[12] When Native leaders tried to represent a dissenting voice at meetings, they were jailed or massacred, like the Lakota at Wounded Knee.[13]

Although Native Americans were originally more populous than the white settlers who invaded their homes, their majority numbers did not save them from the pain and powerlessness of the minority experience. Chief Folsom of the Choctaw tribe describes his peoples' emotional reality well: "We are exceedingly tired. . . . Our doom is sealed. There is no other course for us but to turn our races to our new homes toward the setting sun."[14]

Power is a word that carries many meanings and connotations, but in the context of race, it is most important to understand the following.

There is always a discrepancy between the majority and minority cultures. Sometimes that may mean a difference in perceived ability to act, as measured by Geert Hofstede and Gert Jan Hofstede's "Power Distance Index."[15] Sometimes it's a very blatant imposition of the majority culture's will to restrict the power of a minority group, as in the segregating "Whites Only" signs.

This is where a helpful distinction must be made. *Segregation* is one of the most misused terms in conversations about race and diversity. I've misused the term myself, as when I've referred to ethnic minority groups who form distinct or separate communities and don't mingle with other groups. At times, I still hear employees in Cru and some congregations use the negative connotations of "segregation" to aid their critique of ethnic-focused ministry groups and churches.

However, the European Commission Against Racism and Intolerance defines segregation as "the act by which a (natural or legal) person separates other persons on the basis of one of the enumerated grounds without an objective and reasonable justification, in conformity with the proposed definition of discrimination." Segregation is an act of power imposed upon a minority group against their will, not a voluntary attempt to form a community for support. The Commission's statement goes on to say, "As a result, the voluntary act of separating oneself from other persons on the basis of one of the enumerated grounds does not constitute segregation."[16]

Segregation throughout history has also meant acts of controlling a minority group by intimidation and force. At a gas station, basketball legend Bill Russell's father once was told he had to wait for all the white customers to pump their gas first. After waiting for a long time, he began to leave, but the station owner put a shotgun to his head and ordered him to wait. "Boy, don't you ever do what you just started to do," the white owner told Russell's father.[17] That is racial power.

John Perkins describes how the purpose of the Ku Klux Klan was less about exterminating the black race and more about scaring them back into line. He writes, "The Southern white doesn't want the blacks removed. What he wants is to have the blacks under his control, in a special relationship to him."[18] Thus, lynching was designed as a public spectacle—even publicized in newspapers in order to draw crowds of tens of thousands of people.[19] In each of these examples, there is a vast difference in the power and control possessed (and demonstrated) by whites and blacks.

Differences in power can also be unconscious. Much research on implicit bias shows that most people in the United States have subtle biases about race, ethnicity, age, sexuality, and physical appearance. In the 1940s, African American psychologists Kenneth Clark and Mamie Clark conducted a now famous experiment using black and white dolls to judge the value and beauty young children attributed to race. Overwhelmingly, white children grouped positive attributes to the white doll and negative attributes to the black doll. However, black children were also inclined to attribute goodness and beauty to the white doll and negativity to the black doll. Even at an early age of development, children had internalized value judgments based on the power gap between races.[20]

I attended a lecture by UCLA professor Dr. Miguel Unzueta, who has done extensive research on diversity, bias, and discrimination. Flashing words and images on a screen, and asking the audience to respond with a positive or negative association, he provided a real-time demonstration of how deeply embedded these associations can be. Unzueta and other experts in race studies call this *unconscious bias*—we all possess social stereotypes about certain groups of people outside of our conscious awareness.[21]

Differences in power aren't just between individuals; they are
systemic. The most common term to describe systemic imbalances of power is racial privilege—which in the case of the
United States is white privilege. This means that there are numerous societal advantages from which white people benefit
(e.g., greater access to jobs and housing, social comfort and ease),
even if they're not aware of them.[22]

In *Playing God: Redeeming the Gift of Power*, Andy Crouch
describes the moment he understood privilege and power at an
airport in Mumbai, India. While he waited in a long line of
passengers to be checked in, Crouch was suddenly approached
by the ticket agent, who told him to skip past the seventy-five
people in front of him, straight to the counter. Crouch realized
that his status as a white American male allowed him ease and
access that the other travelers did not have. Though he felt embarrassed and even wanted to tell the others "I didn't ask for
this!" they were not in the least surprised by what had happened.
Crouch notes that *they* understood power and privilege whereas
he was just becoming aware. Indeed, privilege is most invisible
to those who have it.

Crouch defines privilege as "the ongoing benefits of past successful exercises of power."[23] For instance, he got to skip the
line because of America's historical success and accumulated
power. Many people in the world speak English because of
Britain's success in colonizing so many countries throughout
history. As mentioned before, language is a major part of
privilege—when white Americans travel internationally, they

have come to expect that people in other countries should speak English, rather than the other way around. This kind of expectation of convenience is the result of a systemic difference in power between majority and minority cultures.

In my experience, systemic power is often the hardest for people to accept or understand, because it is largely invisible. Also, it is far easier to blame an individual than a system, because a system doesn't have as clear a culprit and solution.[24]

Drew Hart writes about the example of some racially offensive remarks that celebrity chef Paula Deen made, and how quickly she faced backlash from the media. I can think of numerous athletes like Curt Schilling and actors like Mel Gibson who have gotten fired or reprimanded for such remarks. Yet Hart observed that it's easier to blame one person like Paula Deen for being a racist than to face the systemic realities of injustice—the centuries of ideology—that led to her remarks. He writes, "When mainstream America makes an example of Paula Deen, it both turns her into a scapegoat and also creatively claims its own innocence, because it limits the definition of racism to individual acts."[25] It's easier to put the blame on individual acts rather than confronting systemic processes that are broken.

The result of white privilege, and of unconscious and blatant differences in power, is that there are always additional layers that minorities must contend with. Ken Wytsma, author of *The Myth of Equality*, writes, "White privilege doesn't mean your life isn't hard. It means that if you are a person of color, simply by virtue of that, your life might be harder."[26]

In some of my talks on race, I have defined power as *not having to think about something that is significant to somebody else.* Think about it this way. Minorities might have to deal with two or three times as many challenging realities as whites—in the workplace and in everyday social settings. Some whites may *never* have to think about or experience some of these challenges.

For instance, here are some examples of additional layers that minorities must contend with:

- They are often overlooked or go unnoticed, and have to work harder to get noticed, because they are minorities.

- They often have less access and fewer opportunities, because they are minorities.[27]

- They often have fewer people who understand their realities, or who share their experience, because they are minorities.

- They often have to deal with negative stereotypes in the media that devalue their appearance and dignity, because they are minorities.

- They often face discrimination or overt racism, because they are minorities.

In any society, the power disparity between majority and minority cultures inevitably creates these realities. First, living on the "margins" of society comes with certain inherent pressures for minorities. A *New York Times* article about Asian Americans competing for acting roles describes this well. Actress Constance Wu says: "An Asian person who is competing against white people, for an audience of white people, has to train for that opportunity like it's the Olympics. An incredibly talented Asian actor might be considered for a leading role maybe once or twice in a lifetime. That's a highly pressurized situation."

Then if an ethnic minority does receive an opportunity, they often recognize that they are representing their people group to the rest of the organization. A Latina speaker at a conference may not know the next time her people will have a chance for representation, so she needs to make a great impression. A basketball player like Jeremy Lin knows he is the only Asian American athlete of which the public is aware, and so it's on him alone to represent his people. Can you imagine the way these kinds of pressures might wear on a minority?

Second, there's a natural tendency of those in power to abuse it, and this is not unique to the United States. Consider the oppression of Armenians during their brutal genocide at the hands of the Ottoman government in 1915, or the torture and execution of ethnic minorities under the Khmer Rouge regime in Cambodia in the 1970s. These genocides show the extremity of what a power gap between majority and minority can do within a country.

We're not all on equal ground. It's not a matter of whether we like it that way or not, or what we wish it could be. It's reality.

THE PAST

I was horrified and disturbed by the comments sections of sports articles and the racial war of words going back and forth. I also knew most of the people writing were probably a combination of internet trolls and bored people who needed to blow off steam anonymously. But I couldn't stop reading anyway. Have you ever felt the same way?

There were several articles about a talented Latino martial artist named Cain Velasquez and the tattoo he wears across his chest that reads *Brown Pride*. In an interview, Velasquez talked about his challenges growing up not seeing many Latino male role models, and how he took pride in being Mexican and showing the world that people from his culture had strength and dignity too.[28]

But the commenters on these articles took the tattoo in a much different way. Numerous people wrote something of this nature: *If that tattoo said "White Pride" everyone would be up in arms about it. What a double standard! He's the real racist!*[29]

I can't tell you how many times I've heard this kind of argument or sentiment in the past decade. When professional football player Colin Kaepernick refused to stand for the pre-game playing of the United States national anthem, it sparked a heated debate over important topics such as racial inequality, law enforcement violence, the meaning of the national anthem, and respecting the sacrifices of the US military. Kaepernick and his protests even made the cover of *Time* magazine.[30]

In just about every article about these protests, numerous people responded with backlash comments against African American protestors, calling them "brainwashed racists,"[31] "black racists,"[32] and "the biggest racists of all,"[33] and calling Kaepernick's protest "racism in itself."[34]

These kinds of reactionary comments aren't unique to the NFL protests but are commonplace in most discussions on race that I read online, whether on social media or articles about current events.

In a *Los Angeles Times* article that pointed out the concern that white actors were cast to play traditionally Asian roles,[35] some of the responses included: *So the Japanese were racist by making all of their manga characters have Japanese names and Japanese features,* and *When you start getting worked up about black actors playing traditionally white roles then I'll start to care.*

In an article about the insensitivity of the Cleveland Indians baseball team's caricatured mascot (Chief Wahoo),[36] here's a typical response: *Can't the Indians just get over it? I don't call for the banning of "The Jeffersons" on TV because George calls Tom Willis a "honky" as a punch line.*

Perhaps these people were frustrated by the sensitivity to potential racism or discrimination of minorities, and so they lashed out in defense: "Everyone is so sensitive to minorities! If the same things were said about white people, nobody would create such a fuss." Again, these are attempts to equalize things in reaction to assertiveness from minorities.

The problem? We've forgotten about the past.

We all have too short a memory these days. When we look at the simple words of *brown pride* and *white pride*, they seem to be the same, just different colors for different races, right? But the associations are entirely different, and especially when we consider their history.

White pride has historically been associated with (and used by) white separatist and supremacist organizations and individuals, from the Ku Klux Klan to Neo-Nazis. These groups have been responsible for countless murders of ethnic minorities, from African Americans to Jews throughout the world. Their ideology is based in a belief that whites are superior to other races.[37]

Brown pride, on the other hand, is a motto with far less history. If you search for it online, you'll mostly find references to clothing and tattoos, or to Mexican ethnic identity. The most you'll find related to racial violence or tension is a few links to Mexican gangs in southern California. It doesn't carry anywhere close to the same historical association of violence and domination of one race on another as *white pride* does.

The truth is, these terms are not at all the same, not at all on equal ground—when we view them through the lens of history.

A more keen commenter wrote about the Cleveland Indians' mascot debate: "Vikings are a 'people' too. Except the real difference is that Vikings were the conquerors and not the conquered, the oppressed. We, collectively, treated Indians like dirt, like vermin to be hunted, relocated and/or killed. That's the difference." This comment shows an awareness of the way history has impacted the present day. It shows an awareness of power and of the past.[38]

Why do we "forget" the past? Some would argue that this is not accidental, but the result of massive gaps in how we teach and learn about history. In *A Different Mirror: A History of Multicultural America*, renowned history professor Ronald Takaki describes the Eurocentric bias in classrooms across the United States. In what he labels the "Master Narrative of American History," Takaki outlines the "popular but inaccurate story" that our country was settled by European immigrants and that Americans are white. He points out that reputable historians such as Oscar Handlin only studied migrations from Europe and overlooked not only the indigenous Native Americans, but those who were "uprooted" from Africa, Asia, and Latin America.[39]

Takaki believes that this Master Narrative reflects and reinforces the thinking that we see in today's school curricula, news and entertainment media, business practices, and government policies. However, the United States' demographics show that over one-third of its people do not trace their ancestries to Europe. To Takaki, a United States history that contains minorities is not only more inclusive, but more accurate. As minorities get in touch with their histories, they find that they too have deep roots in America's past. As they tell and retell their stories, Takaki writes that minorities "contribute to the creating of a larger memory of who we are as Americans."[40]

During my freshman year at Stanford University, I was required to take a series of classes called "Culture, Ideas, and

Values (CIV)." What I didn't know is that this series used to be called "Western Culture," and was transformed decades before by ethnic minority advocates to be more historically inclusive.[41] If not for that change in curriculum, I would have been exposed even more to the "Master Narrative of American History," probably without even knowing what I was missing! How many of us can say something similar about our history classes from childhood?

Another theory for why whites point their fingers back at minorities and call them racists, is that it's not a matter of historical memory, but of racial reactivity.

Racial reactivity is backlash that goes back and forth between majority and minority cultures, built up by years of mistrust, resentment, and anxiety. Former Attorney General Eric Holder describes this toxic environment like a "powder keg" that can be set off by a single incident.[42]

In her award-winning book *White Rage*, professor Carol Anderson outlines numerous historical examples of white backlash or reaction immediately following a significant advancement for black Americans. For instance, the Black Codes of Mississippi in 1865 outlined severe labor restrictions for newly emancipated slaves, which put blacks at a disadvantage to attain civil rights and economic independence. They had to sign unjust labor contracts, and were forbidden to seek better wages or working conditions with other employers. If they left their work because of intolerable working conditions, they would be jailed and auctioned off. Many historians feel the Black Codes were simply slavery under a different name, but it was a reaction of whites to reassert control that they felt they had lost with the abolition of slavery.[43]

Michelle Alexander comes to a similar conclusion in her acclaimed book *The New Jim Crow*, where she tracks three systems that whites have used for social control—slavery, Jim Crow laws, and mass incarceration. She observes that following each collapse of one of these systems of control, there is a pattern of confusion, transition, and "then backlash intensifies and a new form of racialized social control begins to take hold."[44]

In *Racial Formation in the United States*, Michael Omi and Howard Winant also describe this cycle of minority social advancement, and then a reaction to "reestablish" the identity and strength of the majority culture's place in society.[45] For instance, after the civil rights movement in the 1960s, the state spent money on a range of social programs in the name of equality that left some whites feeling disregarded. In response, they countered with their own cries of "racial injustice" in an attempt to reestablish their place in a changing society.

In reaction to strong civil rights leadership, there inevitably arose strong white identity leadership again in the 1970s and 1980s. The more extreme groups were supremacist movements like Aryan Nations, the Silent Brotherhood, and the Ku Klux Klan—a network of commoners who protested the changes in the federal government. Within the government, leaders like Tom Metzger were backed by more moderate white voters.

One such supporter told a television interviewer, "It's nice to have someone that represents the white people. It seems like nobody cares what the white people say anymore and all the candidates seem to run around and go out to all the minorities and never even once ask the white people how they feel so I guess we're turned around: the whites are now the minority and the minorities are the majority."[46]

How could someone call whites the "minority" in the United States in the 1980s when whites vastly outnumbered ethnic minorities in terms of demographics? *Perhaps statements like the one above have little to do with numbers, percentages, or history—and have everything to do with racial reaction.* After all, whites calling minorities "the majority" or "racists" is the epitome of reactivity. It's the very accusation that they feel is being thrown at them.

It's hard to overstate the power of racial reaction, as it can often overpower and politicize nearly any conversation about race, turning dialogue into accusations and even name-calling. Some of the strongest forces that drive us are subconscious, and have roots from generations long before us—and it behooves us to recognize this today.

THE PAST LIVES IN THE PRESENT

Just around the block in my neighborhood there's a restaurant called Yellow Fever. To many Asians, the term *yellow* has negative connotations because of the way it has been used throughout history to demean their looks or status in society. I must admit that, although I enjoy the food that the restaurant serves, I find it hard to eat there because of the name. But it would be much worse if the restaurant wasn't run by Asians, but by whites.

Many people are familiar with the sitcom *Fresh Off the Boat*—another term that I used to hear in the playground to insult Asian immigrants who didn't speak very good English. Again, the show would be very different if it didn't feature so many Asian American actors but was filled with white people making fun of Asians instead.

Why is this the case?

Why is it that some minority groups can say certain words to one another within their own culture and community? Why is it that when majority culture people use that same word, it's so offensive?

Again we must consider the impact of the past. It's offensive when white people use the word *yellow* or the initials F.O.B., because there is history of whites demeaning Asians or communicating that they don't belong—not just through words, but through events like the Chinese Exclusion Act and Japanese internment camps. Because of the history of racial slurs, the person who's speaking it makes all the difference in how it's communicated and interpreted.

I remember watching an episode of the reality television show *Survivor* when an African American man named Phillip was very sensitive to an older white contestant (Steve) who used the word *crazy* to describe him. Phillip explained the history of words like *crazy* and *boy*, which were used by white people when blacks were enslaved.

The white contestant simply could not understand and kept on insisting that he had "no prejudice" in him. Steve claimed he didn't mean anything other than simply remarking that Phillip had been acting "crazy" like anyone else—regardless of race!

However, no amount of insisting on his intentions could change the associations that came with those words for Phillip. It was another example of how we can't escape the impact of the past. If you're from the majority culture and a minority reacts to a word or phrase that you say, it may have very little to do with you personally. In fact, someone might feel anger or fear—no matter how eloquently or competently you communicate— simply because of what you represent to them as a member of the majority culture.

Of course, that doesn't mean we shouldn't try our best to be sensitive. But we shouldn't forget how much the history of majority and minority dynamics still shapes us today, in ways we feel very strongly and tangibly in our relationships and debates.

As an ethnic minority, I am not part of the white history that drove Native Americans from their lands. However, as a person living in the United States, I share in the benefits of the settlers' actions. I have a home and enjoy privileges based on past and present acts of power of which I am not even conscious. Most importantly, as the late Native historian Jack Forbes once emphasized, I am responsible for the society I live in, which is a product of the past.[47]

What might it look like if the past were acknowledged more often in race-related conversations today? In the debate over professional athletes standing for the United States national anthem, it's a completely polarized choice. Either they must stand and accept everything the anthem stands for, or sit and be perceived as rejecting one's country. What if prior to playing the anthem, someone was to acknowledge the realities of American racial inequality and oppression, and how the song is not a symbol of perfect unity, but of a reminder of how we must continue to strive for justice for all? Can you imagine how powerful something like this could be? How might it speak to minorities, who feel the onus is entirely on them to make an impossible choice between their ethnic communities and the country they love?

In any current race-related event, there is some aspect of history that strongly impacts how people perceive and react to it. That's because the past isn't over and done with. It lives in the present.

GOD'S MESSAGE: "DO NOT FORGET"

You might notice that the three categories of pain, power, and the past are interconnected. It's hard to talk about the past for ethnic minorities, for instance, without talking about pain and power. While there are undoubtedly positive memories as well, a large portion of interracial history between ethnic minorities and the majority culture contain memories of pain—whether it's Native Americans or Latinos being driven from their homeland or betrayed by the breaking of treaties, African

Americans working as slaves and property of their white owners, or Asian Americans always feeling like the enemy because of World War II (internment camps), the Korean War, and the Vietnam War. Many of these events involved the exertion of power from the majority culture to subdue or silence those of ethnic minority communities.

Whether we focus on pain, power, or the past, they all speak directly to the minority experience. They all illustrate the emotional realities that have shaped minorities in a way that a cultural training seminar on ethnic differences and customs simply cannot. They go beyond pragmatic goals and tactics to bring light to the underlying dignity of minorities.

Unsurprisingly, these three categories are not new, but reveal the way that God sees minorities as well. We've already outlined Moses' experience seeing his fellow Israelites enslaved by the Egyptians. The book of Exodus shows us how God heard the cries of the Israelites and delivered them to freedom out of Egypt. However, for the next forty years they wandered in the wilderness, frequently facing famine and other hardships.

In many ways, the Israelites were a minority group—not in terms of their numbers, but in their realities of pain, power, and the past. That shaped God's words to this community as they prepared to enter and finally possess a homeland. He told them:

> Be careful that you do not forget the LORD your God, failing to observe his commands, his laws and his decrees that I am giving you this day. Otherwise, when you eat and

are satisfied, when you build fine houses and settle down, and when your herds and flocks grow large and your silver and gold increase and all you have is multiplied, then your heart will become proud and you will forget the LORD your God, who brought you out of Egypt, out of the land of slavery. He led you through the vast and dreadful wilderness, that thirsty and waterless land, with its venomous snakes and scorpions. He brought you water out of hard rock. He gave you manna to eat in the wilderness, something your ancestors had never known, to humble and test you so that in the end it might go well with you. You may say to yourself, "My power and the strength of my hands have produced this wealth for me." But remember the LORD your God, for it is he who gives you the ability to produce wealth, and so confirms his covenant, which he swore to your ancestors, as it is today. (Deuteronomy 8:11-18)

God's message to the Israelites can be captured in these three themes:

- *Do not forget your pain.* You endured thirst, hunger, and illness because I (God) provided for you. I didn't intend that pain for your harm, but to teach you humility and gratitude.

- *Do not forget that you were powerless.* You were enslaved and oppressed, and I used my power to deliver you. Remember that it's not your own power that creates wealth and safety, but those are in my control.

- *Finally, do not forget the past.* I have been with you from the beginning, and I haven't forgotten the promises I made to your ancestors. Don't lose sight of the big picture, of how I am with you throughout the generations and ages—I have not forgotten you.

God understood the experiences of pain, power, and the past as part of the Israelites' reality—and told them to not forget. Later, he would experience some of these realities himself when he came to earth as Jesus. After all, an order was given to kill all babies under the age of two years, and Jesus had to flee with his family to Egypt as a refugee. He grew up and began his ministry seeing his fellow Jews oppressed under Roman rule.

Jesus didn't just experience the impact of pain, power, and the past—he lived it out in his own ministry to people and the world! He saw people who suffered and were the most marginalized. He advocated for the powerless, and empowered his disciples to lead and serve. Jesus never ceased to remind his followers about history, from the words of the prophets to the ancient promises of God.

As we seek to understand the minority experience in the stories that follow, let's remember that we are not the first to stumble upon these truths and realities—often we need only unlock what is already in the pages of biblical history. Let us continue to draw from the wisdom of the ages, so that we might see with new eyes!

DOMESTICATION

Understanding Power

Can I really be myself?

I'll never forget the feeling of being stared at.

I was at a restaurant in a small town where I hadn't seen any other Asian Americans. My two white friends and I were lining up, waiting to be seated, and I could feel the silent weight of a hundred sets of eyes on me.

It's a very strange phenomenon. There are no words spoken, and *you're not doing anything besides being yourself*—but you know that people are looking at you differently.

My two friends had no idea it was happening, so I had to explain it to them later. I said, "Sometimes I feel like I'm at an exhibition or something . . . like I'm some rare specimen that nobody's seen before."

As a minority, this powerful, silent weight of eyes on the back of our heads puts incredible pressure on us. We desperately want and need to find a way to fit in.

A number of years ago, I coached an Asian American college student named Lee, who felt bothered by some of the power dynamics in his small group meetings. "My white friends keep making jokes about William Hung—you know, the nerdy Asian guy who made a fool of himself during *American Idol* auditions. They make fun of him and imitate his accent," he told me. "It bothers me, but I know that they're just playing around. And they're so nice to me and listen to what I have to say."

I replied, "It sounds like they might simply be unaware of the impact of their jokes, and this could be an opportunity for you to open up, and for them to learn. What would you say if you did speak up?"

Lee paused and then said with conviction, "I would say that the jokes hurt me. I would tell them I see enough negative images of Asian American men in the media, and those are not funny to me. It hurts me that my Christian friends are making jokes in front of me, as if they don't see that I'm there. It makes me wonder if I'll ever really belong."

My eyes teared up as I heard Lee's pain, and I encouraged him to look for a time to share his thoughts and emotions with his group.

A couple of months later, I followed up with Lee to ask how things had gone. "Things are going great!" he said, his eyes lit up.

"So you told your friends how you felt about their jokes, and they took it well?" I asked.

"Well . . ." Lee hesitated. "I haven't really gotten around to that yet. I was going to do it, but my group leader asked me to join the leadership team! Isn't that exciting?"

I smiled, but my heart sank a little. In the months that followed, Lee never shared about William Hung with his group. He had gotten what he really needed, which was to feel accepted. Why take a chance of ruining that—and risking rejection—by confronting his friends?

This experience hit me harder than I thought it would. I had seen that spark of life inside of Lee as he began to get in touch with his dignity and value, and why those were being violated. And just as quickly, that spark was buried under the layers of social pressure, formed by the assimilating power of the majority culture.

I felt sad—because I could relate. Lee's story is my story, too.

WORKING HARDER TO FIT IN

If you're a minority, you might be familiar with a very specific feeling of social uncertainty. You're at work or church, and a group of white people has formed to chat, or to make plans to go to lunch or play basketball. And for just a few seconds as you stand looking at the group, you wonder if you should ask to join them.

Those few seconds of hesitation summarize my childhood.

I was born in New York, but moved around the world quite a bit as a child—from England to Japan. Our family finally settled in diverse southern California, and my parents had about as global of a perspective as could be imagined. My Chinese mother had grown up going to French school in Vietnam, spoke seven languages, and was on my school's multicultural advisory board. My Chinese father grew up in Japan and served as his company's crosscultural guide between the United States and Japan.

You might think with all this rich cultural background I would have been some savant child sharing diverse knowledge and experiences with my friends. In reality, I just wanted to fit in and be like my white friends. So I tried to play American sports, and was the only ethnic minority on my baseball team. I had fun playing, but when everyone went out for burgers or ice cream after the game, I wasn't sure if I belonged with them.

My father was actually the one who enrolled me in baseball and other sports. When he was a child, he remembered being picked on for not knowing who Babe Ruth was. This bullying engrained feelings of shame in him, and doubts about his acceptance in this country—and he didn't want me to experience rejection like he did.

My father had to work hard to fit in when he first immigrated in high school. He was one of only a handful of non-white students at the Massachusetts prep school he attended. Just think about how many stares he received! My father worked day and night reading books on his own to try to improve his English, as well as his knowledge of local customs.

My father and I both experienced a significant reality of the minority experience—the need to work harder than most people to simply fit in because we weren't like the majority culture. We were different.

It's a strange place to be—where being yourself is different, and not necessarily acceptable. I know that sounds like something we've heard before, but stop for a minute and think about it again.

Is it okay for me to be myself?

For many minorities, we have to wrestle with this most basic and fundamental question. We fear rejection. And the reality of rejection is not just "in our heads"!

In 2016, *New York Times* journalist Michael Luo wrote about his experience of a white woman telling him to "go back to China." This motivated him to ask other Asian Americans to write in with their own stories of modern racial insensitivity or discrimination, accompanied with the hashtag #Thisis2016.[1] Here are some of the replies he received:

> My drill sergeants used to tell me in the US Army we are not white black brown or yellow, we are all Army green. Yet when a fellow soldier called me "Private Ching Chong" I had to fight tooth and nail to even convince my superiors that this was a racist comment. I was willing to fight and bleed for my country, was born and raised in this country, yet had to fight to convince them I was as American as they were.—CeFaan Kim
>
> A White lady approached me while I was on my way to my car and said to me, "I hate to see your kind taking the

jobs away from real Americans. Go back to your own country where you belong. We don't need second rate teachers in America educating our youth. Your kind must go back or get shot in the head."—Lui Yuri Lai

Dating as an Asian male, seeing profiles listing preference as "all-American," getting replies like, "No chinks."—Carl Cheng[2]

I routinely got asked on the East Coast: "Where did you learn to speak such beautiful English?" In the NY public schools, just like you. It is a continual reminder that despite being American, in many ways, we will always be "other."—GeriMD, California

As for me, I could add my own experiences to this list. I remember shooting hoops on a basketball court in suburban Massachusetts, when I heard a group of young boys sneer at me, yelling, "Hey, Yao Ming! Nice brick [miss]!" It stung to hear these words, and I felt embarrassed and exposed just standing there. The message I internalized? *All you Asians are the same to me, and it's okay to make fun of you because you look a certain way.*

Luo received an immense response to his #Thisis2016 campaign, and he also decided to write an "Open Letter" to the white woman who had confronted him on the street. In this letter he wrote,

Maybe you don't know this, but the insults you hurled at my family get to the heart of the Asian-American experience. It's this persistent sense of otherness that a lot of us struggle with every day. That no matter what we do, how successful we are, what friends we make, we don't belong. We're foreign. We're not American.[3]

Upon reflection, Luo also wrote, "The tweets struck a nerve with many Asian Americans. It [was] a reflection on 'otherness' . . . this feeling of 'Are we ever going to feel like we belong?'"

Many minorities call this the experience of feeling like a "perpetual foreigner." These feelings come from somewhere. They're not the result of imaginary voices in the heads of minorities, but of actual spoken or written phrases of rejection like "Go back to China" or "No chinks allowed"—in this modern day and age.

These voices of rejection and power are also not new, but have deep roots in history.

DEHUMANIZED

A number of years ago, I met up with a Native American Cru staff worker and friend who told me the story of the Lakota people, whose lands were taken away by white men. As I studied more about Lakota history, it only solidified my conviction that while the minority experience of rejection is psychological, it is shaped by acts of abusive power and exclusion by the majority culture.

I discovered *They Called Me Uncivilized*, the autobiography of Lakota Walter Littlemoon. He recounts how he was forced to attend a federal government boarding school on the Pine Ridge Reservation in South Dakota in the 1950s. The purpose of these schools, which had been created as early as the 1870s, was to convert Native children forcefully to white customs and religion. The motto of Henry Pratt, creator of the "education" programs, was "Kill the Indian, Save the Man."

The first priority of the schools was to strip the Lakota of all aspects of their unique cultural identity. If they spoke the Lakota language, they were hit with belts, sticks, or fists. If they kept any reminders of their home, they were starved as punishment.[4] The other priority of the school was to teach the Lakota the English language and customs, in the hopes that they would become "civilized" and "shaped into the image of the dominant society."[5]

The more I read about these abusive acts of power, the more it horrifically reminded me of the practice of *domestication*—which typically refers to the process by which a person tames an animal. Although I don't believe humans are animals, there was no question in my mind that whites treated the Lakota as less than human beings.

Tragically, this abuse had an impact on Littlemoon's adult life. He writes that many of his Lakota friends took their own lives. Some drank themselves to death, and others "just gave up and didn't care whether they lived or died." As for him, he was scarred emotionally and psychologically. Littlemoon felt guarded and suspicious of others, making it hard to build friendships. He found himself withdrawing to the background and not participating in activities, because he didn't have confidence that he was important and belonged.[6]

Littlemoon writes about how the boarding schools did succeed in stripping away so much of his identity and confidence, which impacted his everyday behavior and mentality:

It seemed to me that our lives had been so firmly shaped by the government boarding schools that we had difficulty making our own decisions. We were always expecting someone to come by and yell at us, and looked at every experience as if it were connected to some rule or regulation. We were always guarded, scared to reach out, and feared being punished. . . . We'd tell the residential manager when we were going out and when we would be returning, though day after day he'd say, "You don't have to tell me." Some of us would stay in the TV room waiting for the manager to turn the set on or to give permission for us to touch the knobs on it; others would never go out except to go to the training. We were so afraid of stepping out of line.[7]

Littlemoon questioned his own value even as he danced with women. He writes, "I'd dance with her in a stiff, awkward way, worrying all the while over what my partner thought. Was she disappointed in my style? Did she want to dance with someone else? . . . Freedom of expression was totally unknown to us. . . . We just sat quietly in a guarded way, for emotional responses had been killed in us."[8]

Littlemoon's story is courageously honest and incredibly tragic. It tells of how human beings in power can treat others without the dignity that all humans deserve, in the attempt to domesticate them; to change them into the image of the dominant culture. History shows that this is not accidental, but actually quite intentional. Native author Randy Woodley describes eugenics, a scientific movement in the late nineteenth century that sought to conform various races to the white model and population, through selective breeding and social engineering.[9] While eugenics eventually lost favor and credibility, it is a clear example of the powerful and purposeful forces that pushed for the domestication of minorities.

Another example of domestication is Japanese internment camps during World War II, when Japanese Americans were "herded" into inhumane living conditions by whites.

In *Farewell to Manzanar*, Jeanne Wakatsuki Houston writes about the day that the Japanese internment camps were closed down and she and her family were free to return home. This day was anything but joyful for her; it was filled with dread as she wondered what her neighbors would think of her, who had become so trained to see the Japanese as enemies. Houston writes, "Three years of wartime propaganda—racist headlines, atrocity movies, hate slogans, and fright-mask posters—had turned the Japanese face into something despicable and grotesque."[10] Moreover, she knew that if someone looked at her with hate, she would have to "take it" because something about her deserved it.[11]

Houston was only ten years old at this time. She couldn't explain the definition of "culture" or define ethnic differences and customs, but she felt the emotional realities of being a minority. Houston did not have confidence that she would be accepted for simply being who she was, and she even wrote that she would have preferred to stay inside the internment camp where she didn't have to face that devastating reality.[12]

Can you imagine that? For many of us, being imprisoned in an internment camp is one of the worst things that could happen. For Houston, however, the internal emotional realities she faced were even stronger than any circumstances from the outside world. For minorities, our challenges don't just stop when our environments change. *We carry around the minority experience with us wherever we go.*

This young girl, like many ethnic minorities, simply wanted to be accepted. However, she grew up with the constant temptation to be more white because she believed the Japanese in her "could not compete with [being white]."[13]

She describes this feeling of longing in heartbreaking fashion:

> I never wanted to change my face or to be someone other than myself. What I wanted was the kind of acceptance that seemed to come so easily to [my white friend]. To this day I have a recurring dream, which fills me each time with a terrible sense of loss and desolation. I see a young, beautifully blond and blue-eyed high school girl moving through a room full of others her own age, much admired by everyone, men and women both, myself included, as I watch through a window. I feel no malice toward this girl.

I don't even envy her. Watching, I am simply emptied, and in the dream I want to cry out, because she is something I can never be, some possibility in my life that can never be fulfilled.[14]

Many minorities actually try to change their appearance to look more light-skinned or white. Eliza Noh, assistant professor of Asian American studies at California State University at Fullerton, describes how her sister got plastic surgery to make her eyes and nose appear more European-looking because she thought her own appearance as a minority was "ugly."[15] There is a boom for plastic surgery in China and Korea, where some clinics perform as many as one hundred procedures a day to reshape eyelids, noses, and faces. Dr. Kim Byung-gun says, "They always tell me they don't like their faces. . . . The Chinese and Korean patients tell me that they want to have faces like Americans. The idea of beauty is more westernized recently. That means the Asian people want to have a little less Asian, more westernized appearance. They don't like big cheekbones or small eyes. They want to have big, bright eyes with slender, nice facial bones."[16]

We want desperately to be accepted for who we are, and this desire is shaped by powerful forces of domestication from the past and present. This is the impact of power on the minority experience.

PREJUDICE OR RACISM?

As the #Thisis2016 campaign showed, minorities still experience racism and pressure to domesticate, or become more white in order to be accepted.

One term used to describe domestication today is *respectability politics*—the pressure from the majority culture for ethnic minorities to speak, look, or act in a certain "respectable" manner (e.g., white). Many blacks in the Ferguson-inspired protests felt that "no matter how well-dressed, well-educated and well-spoken a black person was, he or she was still not accepted by white people in America." Many protestors were resentful of people who shamed blacks for looking or speaking in a certain way.[17] Why couldn't they simply be themselves?

While speaking at a public event in 2016, former football coach Lou Holtz called immigration to this country an "invasion" and declared that minorities need to "become us" (whites). Holtz continued, "I don't want to become you. . . . I don't want to speak your language, I don't want to celebrate your holidays, I sure as hell don't want to cheer for your soccer team!"[18]

Many might call such comments prejudiced or racist, and it may be helpful to define the difference between the terms. Beverly Daniel Tatum defines *prejudice* as "a preconceived judgment or opinion, usually based on limited information."[19]

Racism, on the other hand, Tatum defines as "a system of advantage based on race."[20] Racism isn't just a personal ideology, but a "*system* involving cultural messages and institutional policies and practices." We have seen from our study of the past that this kind of racism was experienced in actual events that dehumanized minorities. Thus, anybody can have personal "prejudice" based on their ideology, but racism chiefly applies to those who benefit systemically from racial oppression.[21]

So does that mean that all white people are racist? Tatum goes on to describe the difference between active and passive racism. Active racism means speaking ethnic slurs and intentionally discriminating against minorities—and certainly many whites do not engage in these kinds of behaviors.[22] However, because racism is so ingrained in the fabric of American institutions and organizations, many of us perpetuate it without even knowing!

Tatum gives the analogy of the moving walkway at an airport. Racism moves along like the walkway, and active racism represents those who walk on the moving platform to go faster still. Passive racism, however, doesn't require more than simply standing on the walkway and being carried forward as unjust ways continue.

Books such as *The New Jim Crow* by Michelle Alexander and *Just Mercy* by Bryan Stevenson detail the existing injustice embedded in our criminal justice and educational systems. Ibram Kendi's *Stamped from the Beginning* traces the origin and evolution of racism throughout United States' history, demonstrating how it's not just a product of ignorance but of a "rationalization of inequity in institutional practices."[23]

To combat racism, Tatum describes how we need to actually walk against the flow of the moving walkway—which takes extra work and effort.[24] It is this systemic view of power and domestication that we must learn to see and understand. It is part of what it means to understand power and the minority experience.

DANIEL AND DOMESTICATION

It is sobering to read of the abuses of power that defiled the image of God in both the oppressed and the oppressors. But it reminds me of a minority who faced similar oppression and domestication efforts in the Bible—Daniel.

Daniel was a Jew living in captivity in Babylon, and he and his friends immediately faced all kinds of attempts to strip them of their culture and religion. The Babylonians changed their names and had them learn the Babylonian language and literature (Daniel 1:4-7). Later on, Daniel was asked to forsake his Jewish diet and refrain from praying to his God (Daniel 6:3-16). It must have been difficult for Daniel to stay true to who he was while remaining respectful of the authorities above him.

Looking at Daniel's choices and life, he did choose to adapt to some Babylonian cultural ways, such as changing his name to Belteshazzar and learning the Babylonian language and literature. He didn't isolate himself, but built relationships with the king's advisors and captains.

While he didn't face abuse in the same way as the Lakota tribe, Daniel and his friends were threatened and tortured, whether it was Daniel's friends being thrown into a blazing furnace (Daniel 3:9-23), or Daniel himself into a den of man-eating lions (Daniel 6:11-16). It was in these times of greatest abuse that Daniel and his friends chose to take a stand against the forces that tried to intimidate them and remain faithful to who they were and to God.

Daniel and his friends believed that no human king had true power, but that power comes from God above, and so he decided to trust in God's power no matter the results. This faithfulness and courage actually endeared the king—and future rulers of Babylon—to Daniel. A later Babylonian king, Darius, made Daniel one of three administrators over the 120 local rulers, and even planned to have him in charge of the entire kingdom (Daniel 6:1-3).

There may be some lessons we can take away from seeing Daniel's story in light of the minority experience. First, there is a difference between adaptation and assimilation. Ethnic minorities undergo a process called *cultural adaptation* whereby we gradually learn to feel more comfortable within a majority-white country or organization. This is normal and expected, and organizations like InterVarsity Christian Fellowship have developed models to guide minorities through the various stages of the process[25]—which can include honeymoon, cultural shock, recovery, and adjustment.[26]

Cultural assimilation, however, has taken on a different meaning than adaptation. In assimilation, a country ideally works toward cultural uniformity (hence the analogy of the "melting pot" of the United States), which means minorities must abandon their culture if they are to be truly loyal to their country of settlement.[27]

Because of this difference in connotation, I've seen language of *assimilation* begin to shift to *adaptation* or even *acclimation*. Regardless of what term is used, it can be helpful for minorities to gain awareness of where we are in our journey of ethnic identity. While it uses the language of assimilation, Kitano and Daniels developed a grid that is widely used.[28] The example of Daniel in the Bible shows that he and his friends had to make choices about where to adapt (changing their names, building relationships), and where to take a stand (diet, praying to God, not worshiping the king, and so on).

There are no easy choices for minorities who face pressure to domesticate. Daniel had to risk his life to be faithful to who he was and to God. In the end, Daniel's integrity didn't cost him his life, but found him greater favor with the king, greater health, and greater influence. But these stories don't always end well.

I see some minorities in organizations wrestle with whether or not to speak up when they sense something is wrong—much like my college student friend Lee. In another instance, I have a Latina friend who was disturbed by the way some of her co-workers were talking about Mexicans on social media during the 2016 presidential campaign. When she confronted her co-workers, there was immediate backlash and attempts to silence her. She even lost some financial supporters because she spoke up. I see this as a case of injustice that my friend was punished financially simply because she expressed her opinions. In fact, she was trying to fulfill God's work and her organization's mission to advocate for the dignity of Latinos.

I've also observed that the many minority staff in Cru that are most outspoken and "raw" about their beliefs are often the ones who take a stand, and ultimately leave the organization. In contrast, the minorities who stay the longest with Cru tend to not "rock the boat" as much.

I've seen this dynamic play out in many other organizations besides Cru, so it's not surprising. However, it makes me sad that the voices we most need to learn from are the ones who feel they can't stay. And often, it's because these minorities feel they have been domesticated and can't truly be themselves.

I believe the challenge for Cru—and all organizations can default to what is most comfortable and safe—is to build enough leaders with the capacity to absorb (and accept) these strong minority voices and perspectives without defensiveness.

Of course, I would never support minorities treating others with disrespect. However, given what we have learned about the history of intense domesticating pressures on minorities, perhaps we need to extend some grace and understanding for the complex emotions that can be surfaced. In my work coaching leaders in Epic Movement, I found that many minorities feel deep anger and sadness in the first couple of years of their ethnic journey, as they uncover emotions that have been buried or suppressed.

Our leadership team intentionally worked to create safe environments, like small groups and online learning communities, for these staff to express their emotions without fear of judgment.[29] In the span of just a decade, we saw Epic Movement grow from twenty staff to well over a hundred. We didn't do things perfectly, but our minority staff knew they could be themselves, and share their thoughts and emotions openly.

After all, if minorities cannot express themselves in the organization, where can they go? They may leave in order to find a place where they feel they can. However, their voices are just as needed as Daniel's was to the king—for the health and flourishing of the organization, and the body of Christ.

TO BE FREE . . .

"I think I hear what you're saying, but I just don't agree."

I was in a staff meeting, and a tall white man next to me had just made a comment I felt was patronizing of minorities. He was a respected and accepted leader in Cru.

He stared at me, and I knew at that moment that I had probably jeopardized my relationship with this man. I felt some regret, but what could I do? I couldn't let his comment pass by in that public setting.

I didn't do it out of defiance or anger. I did it because I believed what I said, and felt it needed to be said.

I did it to be free.

And it felt good and free-*ing* to be myself, apart from any questions about whether this man might harbor resentment toward me for confronting him, or avoid me out of discomfort. After all, that was his choice.

In *Between the World and Me*, Ta-Nehisi Coates writes a wise reminder that history is not solely in the hands of African

Americans, or any minorities. We cannot be responsible for people of the majority culture, as they have their own struggle and choices to make. We can pray and hope for them. However, we are called to struggle, not because it assures us victory—but because there is honor in the struggle itself.[30]

I knew I had made my choice. While I will always be as respectful of my leaders as possible, I will also always choose freedom over some domesticated version of myself. That is how I honor my family and those that have paved the path for me. That is how I honor who God created me to be.

WEARINESS

Understanding the Past

How long can I keep doing this?

Sometimes when I'm in a fairly large meeting of all-white leaders, it can be hard to get a word in edgewise. I must confess that I'm not really an active listener, because I'm formulating my response in my head so it's all ready to go during that one split-second opportunity to interject. I must also confess that sometimes I interrupt someone who's sharing in my attempt to anticipate that split-second opportunity.

I know, it's awful. But in those settings, I fear getting left behind.

It's totally different in a group of ethnic minority leaders, especially in Asian American gatherings. It's not uncommon for there to be a long gap of silence after the first question is asked. There's almost a group instinct to wait and defer. Sometimes it actually leads to long, awkward gaps of silence.

There is space. Even in a larger group of Asian American leaders who are more naturally assertive, everyone generally gets a chance to share if they're willing to speak up.[1]

I don't feel the same anxiety that I do in a white setting. And the more I reflect on it, the more I realize the source of that anxiety. Deep down, I'm thinking, *If I don't say something now, I'll lose my chance. If I lose my chance, I'll get left behind.*

CONSULTING OR INFORMING?

Epic Movement almost got left behind.

For one year, I saw the inner workings of the highest levels of a large, majority-white organization—Cru. I had stepped in to oversee leadership development nationally for our ministry and immediately was in the deep end of the pool. The executive director of our ministry, Tommy Dyo, had decided to step down, and so we were facing the complex issue of finding his replacement. On top of that, leaders in Cru wanted to meet to discuss some "proposals."

I remember our first meeting—sitting in a small hotel room with a handful of white leaders who were highly regarded and among the most powerful in the organization. And here we were, a group of ethnic minority leaders waiting to hear what was going on. Here I was, the youngest and least experienced person in the room by far. What was this all about?

The meeting was very cordial and engaging. We went through a devotional from the Bible, had a good time of personal connection, and then one of our leaders shared some thoughts on some structural proposals that would change Epic Movement as we knew it.

We listened, and then had a chance to ask questions and share any thoughts we had. I remember sitting in the room trying to orient myself and find the right words to share. But the words weren't coming to me. And I remember feeling frustrated by the sense of urgency and anxiety that I felt. After all, these proposals were a complete surprise, and we had no time to prepare for how to respond. I wondered, were my teammates going to speak up and share their concerns? What if we missed our chance?

Before I knew it, our time was up. One of the leaders had a flight to catch. We said our goodbyes and got ready to leave. As we were packing up, though, my teammates looked briefly at one another and asked, "Were they consulting us, or *informing* us?" One person remarked quietly, "It sounds like they've already made a decision."

What could we really do?

Tommy looked at me and breathed a small sigh. "It's nothing new. I've seen this before."

ETHNIC MINORITY HISTORY IN CRU

I sat down to talk with Tommy about the challenges of working as a minority in a majority-white organization. He shared that although he felt supported by Cru, it was challenging how often the organization changed nomenclature, structures, and systems—creating anxiety for ethnic ministries, as well as other ministries. He said, "It's draining for ethnic minority leaders, who are spending their time adjusting to these changes that seem to happen every three to five years in addition to doing ethnic ministry. While I think the heart of Cru leaders is in the right place, things operate at a pretty frenetic pace. They're not going to stop you from bringing your idea, but they're not going to wait for you either. You have to keep up."

But some ethnic minorities can't keep up—they wear down over time. The past takes its toll.

It happened in the 1990s. Over the span of a few years, about a third of Asian American staff left Cru. I talked to a former Cru staff member who watched this exodus happen, and he remarked about the weariness of working as a minority in a majority-white organization. After all, at that time ethnic ministry wasn't sanctioned by Cru as a full-time vocational option— so leaders had to do it as their "second job" after they finished their responsibilities for the greater organization.

For instance, a staff member might work 9 a.m. to 5 p.m. to plan a Cru (majority white) outreach or leadership event. If they wanted to plan any outreaches or leadership events for minorities, they'd have to do that in the evenings. On top of that, they constantly had to defend the validity of ethnic ministry to other people, who questioned why it was necessary to have a "separate" ministry focused on minorities. Needless to say, these ethnic minority staff were exhausted.

In 2005, my former Epic teammate Brian Virtue gathered surveys from minority staff who had left Cru over the previous years, interviewing some of them himself to understand their reasons for leaving. In an article summarizing the results, he concluded, "Staff that feel burdened and beaten down by trying to navigate the organization with very different values and preferences are more likely to leave."[2] While Virtue acknowledged that there are similar reasons why anyone might leave an organization, the difference for ethnic minorities is that this weariness and exhaustion are a *normal* and *ongoing* part of their staff experience.[3]

Because minority leadership is groundbreaking work—and because Western history hasn't included the stories of our cultures—we often don't have the advantage of prior resources to draw on, but must create them ourselves. This comes with great pressure because although we're still experimenting and seeing what works and doesn't, we don't have the luxury of time to do that. Every time ethnic minority leaders fail, we worry that we might get shut down because what we're doing isn't working, and because our work isn't seen as necessary anyway.[4] This can be a very pressurized situation, and weariness usually leads to burnout.[5]

In addition, because we don't have the power or resources of the majority culture, minority leadership efforts are often stretched thin. For instance, at an Epic student conference in January 2013, the ratio of minority staff to students was 1 to 20, while the ratio of Cru staff to students at a corresponding Cru student conference was 1 to 4! Thus, whenever a minority staff leaves the organization, we feel the impact in a significant way. From 2013 to 2014, about half of the Epic leadership development team left, including our leader. These men and women were mentors to me, and had fought for decades for ethnic minority ministry.

An image from the movie *X2: X-Men United* came to my mind at the time. The mutant superheroes are trying to escape a collapsing compound in an airship, and Jean Grey is using all of her powers to hold back the flooding waters that have broken the nearby dam. She is able to save her friends' ship so they are able to escape, but immediately afterward the waters overtake and overwhelm her.

For ethnic minorities, it can feel that the pressures we face from the majority culture are like those flooding waters, and we are trying our hardest to hold them back. Each time one of our coworkers leaves, we feel the additional strain, and wonder, "Will we be the last ones remaining? How long can we hold back the waters?"

MY DECISION TO LEAVE FULL-TIME STAFF

A couple of years after I led our Epic leadership development team alongside my white teammate and mentor, Tom, I decided to leave staff full-time to pursue an organizational development role in the corporate world—and stay part-time with Cru.

In my process of deciding whether to stay full-time or leave, I came to understand the variety of individual and organizational factors that can shape such a decision. There is a life stage factor: many minority Cru staff in their mid-thirties must contend with financial realities and responsibilities, with young children and aging parents to support. Others might want to explore what additional learning and career opportunities are available; studies increasingly show that the work-force of the future is unattached, unconstrained, and values "willing-ness to change" more than financial security or career stability.[6]

Leaving an organization isn't necessarily a bad thing; in some cases, it might be necessary if minority staff find they are no longer aligned with the direction of the organization, or they might need a change to break out of complacency. In my case, I found an exciting opportunity to apply my skills and learn in a new (corporate) environment—while retaining the ability to consult and write about race and diversity as a part-time Cru staff! Weariness is not the only factor for why minority staff leave organizations, but it is a significant one.

THIRTY YEARS OF SILENCE

Weariness is not a new reality for minorities—it comes from the accumulation of challenges from the past. From 1915 to 1970, nearly six million black citizens migrated from the Southern United States for northern and western cities in search of a better life. What motivated them to leave? In *The Warmth of Other Suns*, Isabel Wilkerson describes the wear and tear on blacks who had endured so many setbacks and dehumanizing experiences: "Each year, people who had been able to vote or ride the train where they chose found that something they could do freely yesterday, they were prohibited from doing today. They were losing ground and sinking lower in status with each passing day . . . [many black Americans] saw no option but to go."[7]

Wilkerson details many of the pressures and expectations that African Americans faced in a country where slavery may have been abolished, but systemic racism was still alive and well. She gives the example of Robert Foster, who felt expectations from his parents to somehow make up for all that their family had lost through generations of slavery, and bullying neighborhood kids who resented all that he was able to achieve. On top of that, Foster was constantly reminded that "no matter what he did or how smart he might be, he would always be seen as inferior to the lowliest person in the ruling caste, which only meant he had to work even harder to prove the system wrong because it had been drilled into him that he had to be better than the system construed him to be. He lived under the accumulated weight of all these expectations."[8]

Another example of weariness is Japanese American Fred Korematsu, who was one of the few minorities who challenged the legality of the executive order that interned thousands of Japanese Americans during World War II. He attempted to evade internment, even getting plastic surgery to look more white and changing his name to Clyde Sarah. However, Korematsu was arrested and charged with evasion. Soon after, he agreed to fight his case in court with the help of the American Civil Liberties Union.[9]

Korematsu and his representative Ernest Besig faced incredible political pressure to not take their case to court, given the ACLU's ties to President Roosevelt. Korematsu also faced pressure from the Japanese American community, who didn't all agree with his approach and shied away from interacting with him, for fear of getting into trouble themselves.

Korematsu faced incessant racism, injustice, and dehumanization throughout his life. After he was convicted in court, he and his family were relocated to Utah where he worked at a camp for only $12 a month, and was placed in a horse stall with just one light bulb (talk about domestication!).[10]

No matter how hard Korematsu fought, it seemed he kept facing barriers and roadblocks. While working a job repairing water tanks, he discovered that he had been getting paid only half the wages of his white coworkers. When Korematsu objected, his boss threatened to call the police to arrest him because he was Japanese.

This was the last straw for Korematsu. He quit his job and seemed to lose all hope—remaining quiet for over thirty years.[11] The wear and tear of holding back the dam of injustice had become too much for Korematsu to endure.

Can you imagine what it took to cause an activist like Korematsu to go into silence for three decades? Can you feel the weariness, and the debilitating effects of history?

This is not the end of the story, as in the 1980s, evidence was discovered that showed that certain individuals in the military had lied and covered up information that could have prevented Korematsu's conviction. In 1983, his conviction was overturned and Korematsu gave a powerful statement in court, asking the government to admit its wrongdoing. In 1998, Korematsu was awarded the Presidential Medal of Freedom. On January 30, 2011, the state of California observed a day to remember

Korematsu—the first such commemoration for an Asian American in the United States.

While Korematsu's story ended with some minor restitution, his struggle is a vivid illustration of the minority experience—in the wear and tear of discouragements and abuses he had to endure, and the toll it took on his spirit.

NOT ALONE

It is not easy to resist or act when confronted with the tides of the past. In the Bible, Esther is an example of a minority Jew who had to hide her ethnicity from the Persian king, Xerxes. In addition, she was a woman, and there was recent history of a queen (Vashti) who had made the king angry, such that he issued a decree that all women must submit to their husbands (Esther 1:16-22). Then, the king was manipulated into issuing another edict that ordered the annihilation of the Jewish people (Esther 3:12-15).

Esther must have felt the helplessness of her situation. What could she do in the face of such forces, given the inherent disadvantages of her ethnicity and gender? She had a cousin named Mordecai, but he lived outside the king's court and had little political authority.

Fortunately, Esther and Mordecai did not have to work alone, but became a team. Mordecai mobilized and organized the Jews, and Esther persuaded the king through political shrewdness to issue another edict allowing the Jews to assemble and defend themselves from attack. Royal secretaries wrote out all of

Mordecai's orders to the Jews and to the ruling authorities of the 127 provinces under Xerxes (Esther 8:1-14). Through this mass communication and mobilization effort, the Jews were able to save themselves from destruction.

The past can be numbing, as written history reveals the injustices and the toll of weariness on the minority experience. However, the written word can also be a powerful agent for mobilizing communities.

There was a small moment in history that turned into something much greater. Seven years before the landmark case *Brown v. Board of Education*, a Latino family stood up against segregation at a school in California. The Mendez family created a group called the Parents' Association of Mexican-American Children, and tried to collect signatures for a petition to integrate schools. Many Latinos were afraid to sign because they worked on farms owned by white families and thought they might lose their jobs. Many felt powerless and said, "We don't want any problems."[12]

However, the Mendez family persisted and eventually won their case, setting a precedent that eventually led to the desegregation of schools throughout the country. In 2011, Sylvia Mendez received the Presidential Medal of Freedom. Instead of giving in to helplessness, she fought for justice ("*Cuando la causa es justa, los demás te siguen*"—"When you fight for justice, others will follow").[13]

The Mendez family understood that they were just one voice, and couldn't hold back the dam by themselves—so they mobilized the voices of their people for a greater cause.

When I go on Facebook or social media, I see the power of how quickly and effectively minority communities can form in support of a cause. The "Black Lives Matter" movement originated out of a Facebook conversation. Navajo activist Mark Charles has used petitions to bring change to the steps of the Capitol in Washington, DC.[14] An "Open Letter" by Asian American Christians protesting racial insensitivities in the North American evangelical church was signed by over a thousand people.[15]

Even more, books about race and history continue to be written, and these energize and motivate people to talk and act. While the past carries a spirit of weariness for minorities, it also is a source of life, creative thought, and mobilizing action for justice. Let's keep the books, articles, talks, and movies coming!

AN ENEMY WITHOUT A FACE

The Borg. The Zerg. Stormtroopers. There are so many examples in the media and popular culture of species who pose a "faceless" threat to those who are different. In the case of the Borg from the famous television series *Star Trek*, they relentlessly seek to assimilate other races into a collective mind called "The Hive." Other races are powerless to oppose the process of assimilation, hence the quote "Resistance is futile."

When we consider the wear and tear of history on minorities, it's tempting to want to place the blame on a particular leader, or even on a particular organization. However, I've come to see that many of the systemic realities that oppress minorities are "faceless" enemies. In any large organization that is majority-white, there will inevitably be consistent attempts to assimilate the minority groups or subcultures into the "whole."

In *Organizational Leadership and Culture*, renowned leadership expert Edgar Schein writes about how every organization tends to attract and retain people that fit the culture and assimilate well, while it tends to push out those who do not align culturally. Organizations such as Cru began with a majority-white culture, and for many years this allowed for great success due to its audience and mission in those times. Schein urges that we must understand why the culture of an organization has taken shape:

> Groups are created for a purpose. We huddle together for safety or security or to get something done, and the group's survival depends on the degree to which it accomplishes its purpose. . . . If it succeeds and continues to succeed, the beliefs, values, and behavior patterns that launched the group will become taken for granted as the way to continue. With age and continued success, those beliefs and values will become part of the identity of the group.[16]

We cannot ignore the reality that Cru has been a large and successful organization for many years, with a staff base that is majority white. The inherent message that has settled into the group—whether or not people like it or are conscious of it—is that it can succeed and be secure with its current demographic. That is why so many minorities believe that diversity is treated as optional. In the most blunt and pragmatic sense, diversity *is* optional to many white organizations, because their historical success has not relied on it.

Of course, many organizations are recognizing that this is changing, and they will not continue to grow and succeed without diversifying. Schein writes about how major changes like this are very difficult. First, the culture often cannot be changed directly unless there is a major dismantling of the group or its leadership. Also, when there are changes in the basic assumptions of the culture, it always requires a period of un-learning that is psychologically painful.[17] The challenge for Cru, and many other organizations, is to find and empower future leaders who can help guide the group to overcome some of its constraining cultural assumptions, and resist forces that would sabotage the change efforts.[18]

It is these organizational challenges that we will cover next.

PART 2

REDEEMING THE MINORITY EXPERIENCE

CHALLENGES IN ORGANIZATIONAL DEVELOPMENT

How to Diversify Your Organization

Let's summarize what we've covered so far.

Understanding the minority experience is not so much about demographics or cultural competence as it is about grasping the realities of pain, power, and the past. The impact of pain shows in minorities' psychological sense of self-doubt, while the impact of power can be seen in the rejection minorities experience from a history of white domestication. Finally, the impact of the past can be understood as we grasp the weariness that comes as minorities have had to battle and endure faceless, systemic barriers and injustices.

Most of these realities are heavy and sobering, and I've learned the importance of sitting in the discomfort and pain of this rather than immediately seeking resolution and answers. If your main takeaway is simply the need to better understand pain, power, and the past, I consider that a success.

However, I also believe that the minority experience is not a death sentence or a punishment, but an incredible gift that can benefit those from both the majority and minority cultures.

After all, as I thought about the themes of pain, power, and the past, I realized this:

Leaders who are in touch with *pain* . . . can see and serve people with *compassion*.

Leaders who are in touch with *power* . . . can become incredible *advocates* for the most vulnerable in society.

Leaders who are in touch with *the past* . . . can teach and guide others with great humility and *wisdom*.

In another way of putting it:

Pain builds compassion.

Power builds advocacy.

The past builds wisdom.

A lot is broken in the minority experience. But God did not leave us to be stuck there. He interjects us with new life and the ability to redeem the broken aspects of pain, power, and the past. I think again of Deuteronomy 8:11-18, where God reminds the Israelites that their pain was meant to teach them humility and gratitude. He reminds them to not forget the lessons from the past. And then in Deuteronomy 10:19, God admonishes the Israelites: "And you are to love those who are foreigners, for you yourselves were foreigners in Egypt." He reminds them that God is the defender of the fatherless and widows and loves the foreigners who live among them. God urges his people to remember that they were once enslaved and oppressed as minorities in Egypt, and now they ought to advocate for the minorities in their midst.

When we absorb the realities of pain, power, and the past, we can be tempted to isolate ourselves, but God encourages us to move toward him and other people. We must shift from a self-absorbed mindset to one that sees pain with eyes of compassion, stewards power with hands of advocacy, and reframes the past with a heart of wisdom. In chapters six, seven, and eight, we will explore what this might look like.

Part two of this book is not about simplistic solutions. Professor Soong-Chan Rah reminds us in his book *Prophetic Lament* that United States history tends to be filled with a sense of "triumphalism," which narrates its many victories in wars, economic successes, and inventions of modern conveniences. This lends to a fixation on seeking answers and solutions—when sometimes there are none. Sometimes we can do harm when we try to act, when what is needed is instead to listen, or to lament the injustices that minorities have experienced. Rah writes, "American culture tends to hide the stories of guilt and shame and seeks to elevate stories of success. American culture gravitates towards narratives of exceptionalism and triumphalism, which results in amnesia about a tainted history."[1]

Thus, the following chapters do not always contain a list of actions, but encouragements about when patience and humility are most required, and when we might need to seek help. Or sometimes they include a list of principles or values to guide a healthy process, as in this chapter, where we will discuss leading organizational change in diversity.

LEADING CHANGE IN DIVERSITY: SEVEN STEPS

In *Divided by Faith*, sociologists Michael Emerson and Christian Smith explain how many Christians throughout history failed to confront systemic injustices like slavery and segregation because they tried to solve problems only on an individual level. With this mindset, racial problems could be largely attributed to the "bad apples" of society—the radical, hateful, and ignorant individuals. The solution was for each white person to simply do their best to treat the minorities they knew personally with courtesy and fairness. However, Emerson and Smith outline how this individualistic approach actually has made things worse by ignoring and minimizing the root systemic causes of racial problems.[2]

In this chapter, we will address race and diversity on a systemic level—specifically for organizations that are looking to grow and advance in these areas. Beyond educating individuals in our group, how might we possibly go about a broader change process in a way that is open and honoring? As I write this, I think about Cru's ongoing efforts to restructure their organization, as well as many other parachurch, church, nonprofits, and businesses that are seeking to become more diverse.

Of course, a diversity change initiative should be handled with the same amount of care and intentionality, as any organizational change initiative. As such, I will outline some principles for a change process based on thought leaders in the field of organizational development, interviews with organization leaders, and my own experience in this field.

Step one: Why change or diversify? Before any process is initiated, our motives must be clear. If we're only seeking to diversify for tactical or pragmatic reasons, we won't truly benefit from all that minorities in our organization have to offer. They will simply be a means to an end, and we will treat them in tokenizing ways. Pain, power, and the past are markers for us to assess whether our organization is truly willing to go deeper than "cosmetic diversity."

- Are we willing to listen and absorb stories of *pain* from minorities in our organization?

- Are we willing to confront imbalances and abuses of *power* in our organization?

- Are we willing to explore the impact of *the past* in the United States and in our organization?

Step two: Who will lead our change process? This is the most critical element. Too often, I've seen organizations work on getting the right tactics or strategy in place, without considering that successful change is more about getting the right people to lead the process. Patrick Lencioni, a popular author and expert on organizational health, emphasizes in his books repeatedly that "the single biggest factor determining whether an organization is going to get healthier—or not—is the genuine commitment and active involvement of the person in charge."[3]

So who are the right people? Edgar Schein describes a few qualities of a change leader:

- She has the capacity to perceive and think about ways of doing things differently from the organization's current assumptions.

- She is able to operate on the margins of the organization, while staying connected enough to its core.

- She is able to listen and to absorb difficult realities and assess implications for the organization and what they will require of people.

- She is able to seek and accept help, and is willing to experiment and even fail.

- She is able to acknowledge complexity, and has the emotional strength to admit uncertainty.

- She is able to build the organization's capacity to learn.[4]

To this list, I would add that an ideal change leader must be patient and have the capacity to tolerate ambiguity, and must be able to take a stand when necessary and not let a few voices sabotage or undermine the process.

Other qualities may vary depending on the organizational context, but usually this change leader has some history, trust, and authority within the organization.

Once a leader is identified, she should form a team of change agents to support the process. Of course, team members should possess some of the same qualities as described above. Brenda Salter McNeil, director of the Reconciliation Studies program at Seattle Pacific University, writes in *Roadmap to Reconciliation* that this team should also be diverse itself: "If an organization wants to shift its cultural identity, it is crucial that it have an internal team of diverse leaders who model the diversity change initiative. The leaders thus serve as a microcosm of what is hoped for in the broader community."[5]

Diversity can mean categories like ethnicity, gender, and socioeconomic class—but teams can also benefit from a mix of experienced employees and those who are new to the organization. It is not possible to include a person of every conceivable category; what is more important is that the people on the team are collaborative enough to include a variety of people in their research. As Lencioni points out, inclusivity "should be achieved by ensuring that the members of a leadership team are adequately representing and tapping into the opinions of the people who work for them, not by maximizing the size of the team."[6] An ideal team size is somewhere in the range of four to seven people.[7]

The team leader's job is to align this team with their goal and role, which includes providing ongoing feedback on why new solutions may or may not work, and bringing back concerns they hear to the team.

At this point (and at every following step of the change process), it is also helpful to communicate about the process to the organization: what is being done, who is involved, and why.

It is generally suggested not to call the effort a generic "change process," but to specifically describe the initiative (e.g., diversity and inclusion) and how it is tied to the needs and future of the organization.

Now is also the time to let people in the organization know that the team will be seeking their input and feedback along the way.

Step three: Make an organizational assessment. Before the team does anything, the first step is to assess a couple of things:

What is the current culture of the organization in respect to diversity? What is its history? Schein notes that many change programs are initiated by those who don't have a deep and demonstrated understanding of the existing culture of the organization. As a result, the program does not connect with the needs and language of the organization, and it has difficulty being implemented.[8] The team must take the time to deeply understand why the organization is the way it is, and what kind of history has caused this. Schein provides the well-known categories of (1) artifacts, (2) espoused beliefs and values, and (3) basic underlying assumptions to help in deciphering an organization's culture.[9]

To what extent is the organization motivated or ready to change? It is tempting to think that we possess the power to change with our hard work, strategies, and persuasive methods, but McNeil observes that in her work with organizations, the "most powerful ways we change are often out of our control."[10] She finds that most people and groups need a "catalytic event" to jump-start a process of change.[11] Schein outlines a whole list of unplanned factors that can create an environment conducive to change, from crises to major changes in technology and personnel.[12]

The important thing to note here is that when we are fully aware of the factors that are within *and* out of our control, we are better able to calibrate our expectations. What will be required of us, and what do other people need to do? How long will this process take? What kinds of barriers and roadblocks might arise along the way?

Also, we are able to make any necessary adjustments in our approach. For instance, Schein describes how most organizations and individuals are inherently resistant to change, because change creates *learning anxiety*—the extra work, insecurity, and ambiguity that inevitably comes with a new reality. To address this, a leader or team must seek to create enough *psychological safety* for the organization that it reduces this learning anxiety.[13]

Ultimately, this step of assessment is valuable not only to understand the organization, but for the group to develop its own identity and learn to work together effectively. A team should ideally be given enough opportunities for reflection, process analysis, and informal activities before diving into total task engagement.[14]

Step four: What is the goal and problem? Too many teams, work groups, and task forces work on answers or solutions without first identifying the real problem. Emerson and Smith describe the "constant sense of urgency" that drives many organizations that don't end up asking the right questions because they haven't adequately thought through the issues.[15] Lencioni calls it "the adrenaline bias." He writes that leaders are "seemingly hooked on the daily rush of activity and firefighting within their organizations. It's as though they're afraid to slow down and deal with issues that are critical but don't seem particularly urgent."[16]

Instead of rushing into action or solutions prematurely, we must take the time to do careful reflection and proper inquiry. What is the problem, and what is our goal when it comes to diversity? We should spend the majority of our time determining these. Here are a few ideas and guidelines in doing this:

- Gather existing research on diversity. What are the gaps in the organization, qualitatively and quantitatively?

- Interview minorities in the organization, as well as white leaders who have worked under minority leadership. Some examples of questions include:
  - What is most important to them?
  - What are their biggest challenges and barriers?
  - What kind of support and help do they most need?

- Interview people outside the organization, especially those who have thought through diversity quite a bit. Learn from their biggest challenges and best practices. These perspectives will help fill in our natural blind spots, as large organizations tend to lose touch with reality because of a dominant "internal focus."

- Synthesize your learnings, find themes, and then seek to discover the potential root cause. Tools like the fishbone (Ishikawa) diagram can be helpful in digging below the surface to uncover the cause of issues.

- At this point, your team should be able to come up with a clear goal. This goal should address the root cause of the problems related to diversity. Get some feedback from people in the organization, and make any adjustments that are necessary. Communicate with the organization about progress.

Now that we're at the point of discussing tactics, it may be helpful to share an example of a recent change process within Cru that I believe was handled well. It was a complete restructuring of Cru's International Graduate School of Leadership (IGSL) in the Philippines, which involved one hundred administrative staff and faculty serving a body of over three hundred students from countries such as Bhutan, Sri Lanka, Laos, Congo, and Bangladesh. IGSL conducts leadership training in many diverse contexts including some branches of the Philippines government and military, many businesses, and the homes of pastors' wives in rural Thailand and Sri Lanka.[17]

I interviewed Brian Virtue, who helped oversee change at IGSL as Director of Leadership Development and Human Resources, and also as the interim executive director of the school. To provide some background, there were several factors that created an openness to change when Brian first started serving at the school in 2013. First, most of the school's executive team and half of the faculty were between the ages of 58 and 63, and thus there was a natural urgency to find leadership successors. Second, it had been over a decade since the school's last curriculum revision, and there hadn't been many new faculty from outside the school in a long time, so many felt it was time for new perspectives. Finally, there was a growing sense of leadership problems that the school felt needed to be addressed, including gaps in developing people, holding them accountable, and unrealistic job descriptions.

Over the next few years, there was an influx of ten to twelve staff and faculty from outside the school, and even outside Cru. A task force of five people was created to address the school's biggest needs and gaps. This team was intentionally created with ethnic and gender diversity, as well as diversity of newer and long-tenured staff. Each member of the team had a collaborative mindset and some significant experience in organizational development work.

This team interviewed the faculty at the school, and did research into its biggest gaps, and these came to be known as the school's "Four Cultural Commitments": accountability, development, collaboration, and capacity (overworking of staff).

Step five: Prepare for change. This critical stage involves laying the groundwork for change in the organization. McNeil calls this the "preparation" stage.

Knowing that organizational restructuring was a school goal, the IGSL task force worked to prepare staff for the big changes to come. They had all staff and faculty take a survey to identify their strengths, personalities, and interests. They also asked half of the faculty to undergo 360-degree feedback surveys. These processes allowed the leadership team to collect a lot of data that they could use in order to help with placement (job assignments) in the case of a restructuring. Having this data on hand allowed them to demonstrate that the process was driven by data as opposed to favoritism.

The preparation stage also involves a lot of trust and relationship building. Since Virtue and his family lived in close quarters with the staff and faculty, it helped that they were accessible. This helped them learn culturally and adjust to living in the Philippines, and it also built mutual trust. This relationship building is not only critical between whites and minorities, but it also helped as Virtue and other members of the task force needed to engage in difficult conversations with people who needed time and space to process the organizational restructuring, and its impact on their jobs and families.

Sometimes this "preparation" stage can take a while. Paul Tokunaga is the author of *Invitation to Lead* and coordinated InterVarsity Christian Fellowship's Asian American Ministries for fourteen years. He told me about a leadership meeting he attended in 2003 where he proposed a minority leadership development program called the Daniel Project with an audacious goal. The vision was that in the next decade, the program would build minority leaders who had the capacity to lead the organization at the highest levels, including the president of InterVarsity!

The three goals of the program were for minority staff to (1) grow in their ethnic identity, (2) understand the organization better at senior levels, and (3) own and navigate their own career trajectory. Each participant was assigned a mentor (who was paid, and usually an ethnic minority) for at least a year.

Increasingly, organizations are turning to leadership cohorts or "Business Resource Groups" to provide communities of support for ethnic minorities or women. They provide mentors, bring in outside speakers, and allow space for leaders to develop peer relationships with those who share similar realities.[18]

As for Tokunaga's proposal of the Daniel Project, its vision of building diverse leaders who could step up to the highest levels of organizational leadership seemed outrageous at the time. However, after the program's first year, twelve of its fourteen participants were promoted within the organization. Then in 2016, InterVarsity appointed the first nonwhite president in its seventy-five-year history, Taiwanese American Tom Lin![19]

Though this is encouraging change, Tokunaga told me that it took years of building trust to open ears to proposals like this. He had been part of InterVarsity for thirty years, and had many conversations that led to this moment. Preparing the groundwork for change takes patience, and InterVarsity knows there is still work to be done to support other minority leadership cohorts and women of color.

Step six: Execute change. You may notice that the change process outlined here is intentionally broad in its scope. Too often, diversity initiatives are simplified to training classes or delegated to one department (e.g., Diversity and Inclusion). This approach not only can inhibit organization-wide collaboration, but it risks treating diversity as an optional side project, as opposed to an element that should influence every process and department.

For instance, diversity should impact marketing strategies, recruiting and hiring, onboarding, leader training, performance reviews, leadership selection and promotions. By integrating and embedding the diversity change process throughout the organization, this will give the best chance to shape culture—and build the capacity of the organization to sustain it.

As specific tactics of the change strategy are executed, there are at least four activities that one should be prepared for:

1. *Change-related meetings.* For the IGSL, this meant gathering more experienced leaders in the school for reflection and vision on how to effectively pass their legacy on to the next generation of leaders. It meant facilitating meetings for the staff to talk specifically about how they were processing transition-related matters. For faculty that were stepping out of their positions, the school held meetings for them to share their journey and learnings with others, and to honor and celebrate them.

2. *Change-related side conversations.* In most situations, there will be individuals who will mostly feel free to talk about

their concerns or fears in "side" conversations (i.e., not during official meetings or gatherings). Thus, leadership must be prepared to be involved in responding to any perceived anxieties, and even to proactively check on people individually. This work is some of the most important, though it will often be the most informal in structure and timing.

3. *Change-related communication and feedback.* Again, during the transition process, there needs to be consistent organization-wide communication, and the opportunity for people to provide meaningful feedback. Lencioni believes that when it comes to reinforcing clarity, there is no such thing as too much communication.[20] He points out that too many leaders see communication in a cognitive manner—as the mere transfer of information to an audience, which can seem to become redundant. Instead, Lencioni suggests a more relational, emotional view of communication. This involves connecting with people, reassuring them, and helping them to understand, internalize, and embrace the message. He writes: "The only way for people to embrace a message is to hear it over a period of time, in a variety of different situations, and preferably from different people."[21] Consistent communication is vital.

4. *Capacity building for long-term sustainment.* McNeil writes that when many organizations experience the instability that comes with change, it becomes too painful for them,

so they abandon the process. She encourages organizations to anticipate instability as normal, and urges change agents to work to build structures that support long-term sustainment.[22] In the case of IGSL, they completely restructured the school and redrafted job descriptions for almost every position, and one can imagine the anxiety that could have emerged in this situation! However, the leadership team intentionally structured a period of only three months of uncertainty—after which every staff was placed in a position based on their preferences, organizational needs, team chemistry considerations, and survey and 360 data. The new job descriptions and a newly defined organizational structure provided clarity, and the change team communicated regularly with the staff and faculty. Throughout the process, they provided opportunities for the "old" and "new" guard to provide feedback and input.

Step seven: Internalize change. In the final step of the change process, leaders should continue to communicate to remind people of the original goal so they can internalize the meaning of the changes they are observing. They should also reinforce the values of the process—it's not just pragmatic results—so that the organization sees the intentionality of the means by which things have been done.

As people begin to see and experience these new realities, they will gradually adjust. Some may not, or it may take longer, but if leadership shows care, detail, and intentionality throughout the process, that's what will make a bigger difference than expecting everybody to like or agree with the changes.

With IGSL, Virtue told me that when change is successful and people begin to see results, they may want to give more permission to the change team to push the boundaries in other areas. One should take care to steward this power and not pursue more change than the organization can handle. Again, this requires the ability to discern the emotional state of the organization, to have the restraint to provide the right amount of psychological safety and the patience to wait for the right timing.

In the end, the IGSL underwent a successful restructuring and change process, which is no small feat given the scope and the cultural factors and traditions of the school. Virtue attributes this to a mix of unplanned factors (which he attributes to the work of God), timing, the right mix of leadership and values, and most importantly the humility and character of the elder leaders of IGSL—who were more committed to the future of the organization than preserving their own positions, titles, or "ways of doing things."

This process is not far from the "Four Disciplines" model that Lencioni outlines in *The Advantage*, which involves four steps:

1. Build a cohesive leadership team (get the right people to lead the process)

2. Create clarity (define the goal and problem)

3. Overcommunicate clarity (communicate change through preparation, meetings, and side conversations)

4. Reinforce clarity (solidify the results by reminders)[23]

In any change process, there are factors in and out of our control. But if we follow some of the principles above, we will have built a collaborative process that relies on the character and capacity of leaders—which is the most important measure of success.

SEEING PAIN WITH EYES
OF COMPASSION

Does anyone see me, or am I invisible?

I was confused. In the big auditorium where five thousand staff were gathered, I looked over at two of my coworkers in the seats next to me. They were in tears. I had no idea what was happening, because all I had heard from the speakers on stage for the past thirty minutes was encouraging updates about their ministry. What could have made my friends so upset?

Every two years during July, Cru puts on a conference at Colorado State University where their United States–based staff gather for connection, learning, and worship. It's quite an impressive production: huge television screens, skits, speakers like Tim Keller and Francis Chan, and even Christian bands like Rend Collective and Tenth Avenue North.

This conference is also quite a phenomenon for minorities, as the attendees are over 85 percent white. I still recall when one of my local Colorado friends who visited a session remarked,

"I've never seen this many white people in one room before." It can be a shock for those who live in more racially diverse places in the world.

But minorities can feel "invisible" in ways other than demographics. As I turned to ask my coworkers why they were crying, I learned that a painful experience in their organizational past had just been spun into a positive report by the speakers up front at the conference. As a result, they felt unseen by the organization and their leaders.

It then struck me:

Positivity can be blind.

Pain sees.

THE BLINDNESS OF POSITIVITY

Over the next couple of conferences, I noticed there seemed to be an organizational commitment to share mostly uplifting stories of progress and success. On one level, it made complete sense. I mean, who goes to a big rally only to walk away depressed and sad? However, over the years I started to sense a frustration and hopelessness from the minority community, and finally I started to get it.

It wasn't that minorities didn't want or like the positivity of the organization. They were more bothered by the seeming refusal to address difficulties, challenges, mistakes, and oversights. After all:

- When the organization didn't address challenges, it didn't see or acknowledge the unique realities many *minorities* faced—pioneering, fundraising in new ethnic communities, and so on.

- When the organization didn't address mistakes, who were the ones these mistakes had most impacted? *Minorities.*

Put another way: by refusing to acknowledge pain, the organization also refused to see or acknowledge the *people* in the most pain—minorities.

After all, pain is a very important part of reality. If organizational conferences and leaders don't publically and consistently acknowledge pain, they can quickly become out of touch with reality, and with minorities who must constantly navigate additional layers of pain and complexity. And if minorities continue to feel invisible in this way, they may question their fit or place in the organization.

Of course, this dynamic of *blind positivity* has happened throughout history. I am fortunate to have two daughters, and my oldest is currently in elementary school in southern California. She had to do a report on American history, detailing the journeys of Christopher Columbus to the New World. In the paragraphs she had to read, there was no mention of the many unjust ways that Columbus treated the Native American people he encountered—from putting them into slavery to brutal violence to trying to convert their language and religion.[1]

While some may consider these details inappropriate for children to learn, it reminded me that even at age six, minority children are learning the (inaccurate) "Master Narrative of American History." Indeed, in *An Indigenous People's History of the United States*, Native American activist Roxanne Dunbar-Ortiz calls this the "Columbus myth and the Doctrine of Discovery," because Columbus didn't discover anything—the Native Americans were already there![2]

I was struck that I never heard this side of history even as I got older. Instead, I went through middle and high school playing "educational" video games like *The Oregon Trail*, where the hero of the game is a white settler who journeys West amid the excitement of open territories and new technology like the railroads. I didn't hear about Plains Native peoples (e.g., Pawnees, Sioux, Cheyenne) whose way of life was decimated by the hunting of the buffalo and the transformation of the prairies by new technology.

Dunbar-Ortiz describes the brutal history behind many terms that are used insensitively today. For instance, the Washington Redskins are a popular football team, but many believe the term "redskin" was used as a name for mutilated and bloody corpses of Native Americans that whites left in the wake of scalp-hunts.[3]

I played games like *The Oregon Trail* without even thinking about or questioning the history behind it. Native Americans were invisible to me. How many other minorities have been forgotten by history? I think of the Chinese workers who were recruited to build the First Transcontinental Railroad and the Central Pacific Railroad. They were used for the job because it was cheaper: the construction companies paid them less and wouldn't pay for their board or lodging. These Chinese workers were exposed to such dangerous working conditions that thousands lost their lives due to explosions and avalanches. Yet who remembers and tells this part of history?

For the majority culture and those in power, it's easier to stay "positive" and talk about the peaceful Indians and wonderful stories about the pilgrims and Thanksgiving. It's easier to talk about how intercontinental travel revolutionized the economy and settlement of North America. Yet for minorities like Native Americans and Chinese Americans, this portrait of history ignores them and makes them invisible.

It doesn't have to be this way. Through books like Dunbar-Ortiz's and *Living in Color* by Randy Woodley, many historical details are filled in to help us to understand, and to remember. I'll never look at games like *The Oregon Trail* or watch a Washington NFL game in the same way again.

During Cru's conferences in 2015 and 2017, I noticed that there was a concerted effort to address challenges, mistakes, and pain—and with some special attention given to crosscultural relationships and dynamics. The speakers and panels gave space and voice for minorities to share some of their struggles. On the campus where the conference was held, there were posters with quotes from minorities sharing the hardest parts of their experiences at previous conferences. It made a difference for me, as I felt that my pain as a minority was more seen and heard. I didn't feel as invisible.

Other organizations such as InterVarsity Christian Fellowship, CCDA, and Lausanne have also led the way in terms of diversifying their platform speakers, content, and worship. These are some of the many attempts to give voice to minorities so they can be heard, seen, and valued for who they are.

THE BLINDNESS OF NEUTRALITY TOO

It's not only positivity that ignores pain, however. Perhaps an even more prevalent challenge in today's dialogue about race is the idea of *colorblindness*, or the idea that it is better not to talk about or highlight race at all. Sarah Shin's *Beyond Colorblind* points out that when we neglect talking about race, we unwittingly give permission to the status quo, which, for example, teaches more about white history than Native American history. In order words, we drift down the "moving walkway" of passive racism.

Shin writes that when we are colorblind, we actually are blind to certain people and not others. When we tell a minority "I don't see your color," what they hear is "I don't want to hear about good parts of who you are . . . and I don't want to walk with you in the pain of what you have experienced."[4]

Silence is not neutral in an unjust society. In a speech at a Michigan high school in 1968, Martin Luther King Jr. confronts the myth that time is neutral and thus we need to simply be patient with issues of racial justice. He says that the forces of ill will and injustice are much stronger than those of good will, and he bemoans the "appalling silence and indifference of the good people who sit around and say [to] wait on time." Rather, King says that progress comes only through the persistence of dedicated people who partner with God.[5]

Neither time nor history are neutral. If we don't have eyes to see pain, we perpetuate the invisibility of the minority experience.

THE GOD WHO SEES US

Pain isn't easy to see. As discussed earlier, minorities often internalize our pain, which takes the form of shame and self-doubt. We believe we are unworthy, and when we believe that, it is much harder to see others as worthy. We can become so isolated and absorbed in our own pain that other minorities are invisible to us.

But God does not see us as unworthy. Zephaniah describes how God takes "great delight in" people, so much that he rejoices over them with singing. This tender image is coupled with language of justice and action. God says he sees those who have been oppressed, and will rescue those who have been exiled. He promises that he will give the marginalized praise and honor "in every land where they have suffered shame" (Zephaniah 3:17-19).

In the book of Genesis, when Abram's wife Sarai mistreated her Egyptian slave, Hagar, and Hagar fled into the desert, God sought Hagar out and found her. God promised to bless her, and honored her so much that she said, "You are the God who sees me" (Genesis 16:1-16).

Jesus, too, saw and associated with the outcasts of his society. He surprised his disciples by talking at length with a woman from Samaria—a minority region of Israel with which many

Jews refused to associate (John 4:1-42). Jesus was criticized for associating with the marginalized—he even included a disregarded tax collector, Matthew, in his group of twelve disciples. In response to the criticism, Jesus told this parable: "Suppose one of you has a hundred sheep and loses one of them. Doesn't he leave the ninety-nine in the open country and go after the lost sheep until he finds it? And when he finds it, he joyfully puts it on his shoulders and goes home" (Luke 15:1-7). Jesus illustrates that the heart of God is not about numbers or percentages, but about seeing the value of each person—especially those who have been overlooked and mistreated by society.

When we accept that we are seen and valued by God, it can change everything. After talking to Jesus, the Samaritan woman went back to her town to tell everyone about her conversation. As a result, an entire town of minorities went from "invisible" to following Jesus. The disciple Matthew—once a despised tax collector—becomes one of Jesus' ambassadors to not only Jerusalem, but all of "Judaea and Samaria, and to the ends of the earth" (Acts 1:8, 12-14). Matthew was once himself invisible, but now his mission is to see and bring healing to many other people who have been overlooked. When we encounter the love of God and people, our pain can build our compassion for others.

One powerful story of two people who saw one another's pain is found in the book of Ruth. When Ruth's mother-in-law, Naomi, suffered the devastating loss of her husband and two sons, Ruth saw Naomi's pain and decided to accompany her back to Naomi's home town of Bethlehem. This was a huge sacrifice for Ruth, who was from a minority region of Israel called Moab, and as a minority chose to enter a land where she would likely be invisible.

However, many scholars overlook the notable act of compassion and sacrifice that Naomi extended toward her daughter-in-law. In *The Gospel of Ruth*, Carolyn Custis James describes how Naomi was at rock bottom with no social status, as she faced the dual curse of widowhood and infertility. In a male-dominated society, Naomi had no source of income, no future family heir, and no male protector against those who prey on widows.[6] In the face of this despair, Naomi still had two daughters-in-law who were culturally duty-bound to her by marriage. She went against convention when she released Ruth and Orpah from this duty, urging them to return to their ancestral lands. James calls this an act of selfless compassion, which is captured in the Hebrew word for sacrificial love, *hesed*: "In the act of emancipating her daughters-in-law, Naomi is herself displaying *hesed*, for she is voluntarily putting their interests, their futures, their happiness ahead of her own desperate need for assistance and companionship. Hers is the first great loving sacrifice in the book."[7]

Ruth's actions and sacrifice are detailed throughout *The Gospel of Ruth*, and James does a masterful job showing how radical Ruth's decisions were in a patriarchal culture such as Israel. It is quite a statement when the women of Bethlehem told Naomi that Ruth was better to her "than seven sons" (Ruth 4:15). Moreover, we learn that Ruth's son Obed would go on to build the royal house of King David that ultimately produced the long-awaited Messiah. Ruth—an ethnic minority woman—brought visibility to Moab, to Naomi, and to the town of Bethlehem. But we cannot forget about the act of compassion of Naomi, who saw the pain of what Ruth might experience as a minority—and who was willing to sacrifice her own future to release Ruth from those painful realities. Pain, through the love of God and people, can build our compassion for others. Pain can help us have eyes to see.

Lawyer and author Bryan Stevenson—who has seen many of the worst abuses and injustices in the criminal justice system—writes that "there is a strength, a power even, in understanding brokenness, because embracing our brokenness creates a need and desire for mercy, and perhaps a corresponding need to show mercy. When you experience mercy, you learn things that are hard to learn otherwise."[8]

In *Embracing the Other*, Grace Ji-Sun Kim writes, "The marginalized and downtrodden receive special insights. They are the ones who can see the pain and injustice that are killing the world. It is to these voices that we must turn."[9]

LEARNING TO SEE

So where do we go from here? What might be some examples of learning to move from a place of pain, invisibility, and self-doubt to a place of compassion?

First, we must take care not to try to minimize or soften pain. Pain is inherently uncomfortable, and as such we will be tempted to avoid it or sugarcoat it. In *The Cross and the Lynching Tree*, activist and theologian James Cone tells the brutal story of Emmett Till, a fourteen-year-old African American boy who was beaten and lynched in 1955 Mississippi. Till's mother insisted that the sealed casket be opened for a three-day viewing to the public so that people could feel the pain and injustice of what had happened.[10] Jesus' followers had to endure seeing their beloved leader beaten and executed, and then put in a grave for three days, before there was any resurrection or hopeful thought of action. Just as there is no resurrection without death, there is no compassion without pain. Jesus taught that sinners who have been forgiven often possess the most love, while "whoever has been forgiven little loves little" (Luke 7:47). We must feel the pain of the minority experience before we can build the compassion to see those who are invisible.

Second, we must be patient and slow to condemn ourselves and others when it comes to racial sight. When I began my own journey of understanding what it meant to be a minority, I was filled with mixed emotions: anger, sadness, but most of all confusion. I was self-absorbed, and all I could see for a while was my own pain and reality; I was a far cry from being able to see other minorities' painful realities, many of which were far more traumatic than mine!

This is not unusual. In February 2012, Taiwanese American Jeremy Lin made a huge splash in the NBA, leading the struggling New York Knicks to seven consecutive victories. This created an incredible buzz among the sports media, as well as through social media among the Asian American community, that was soon called "Linsanity." I remember this particular month like it was yesterday, and it was surreal. Every other night, I would turn on ESPN's *Sportscenter* and see Jeremy Lin's face and game highlights as the feature story at the top of the hour. Every time I would log in to Facebook, my newsfeed was dominated by hundreds of posts and articles about Lin. I joined a team of fellow Asian American Christian bloggers at the website Next Generasian Church to write about Linsanity, and our posts together broke the all-time readership record of the site—interest in our minority community was at an unprecedented high![11]

In a sport with almost no Asian American representation, Jeremy Lin had moved from "unnoticed" (as Kobe Bryant described him[12]) to one of the most popular athletes in the media.[13] Influential blogger Phil Yu of angryasianman.com expressed the significance of Lin well: "There's a certain validation to this. . . . Asian Americans are still seen as foreigners in this country. Seeing Jeremy Lin accepted and celebrated in this American sports, it makes us more American, and it makes other people see us as more American."[14]

PEOPLE ARE NOT STRATEGIES

One way that organizations can unknowingly treat minorities as "invisible" is by treating them transactionally, as a strategy. There's nothing wrong with listing ethnic diversity as an organizational priority. However, the bigger question is, Do we see the *people* behind our agenda or strategies? Would we focus on diversity, even if it wasn't clear how it had immediate tactical value? After all, as a minority I long to know that I have inherent value, and I am not just a number on a spreadsheet or graph that gets reported to a CEO. Organizations must ensure that minorities do not become invisible when we don't happen to fit into their current strategic plan.

But what was all of this like for Lin himself? In an interview that he gave later, Lin shared that he struggled with all the attention that came with being one of the first Asian Americans to play in the NBA and with having to carry the expectations of a minority community that had been underrepresented and stereotyped for so many years. He confessed that he felt scared, overwhelmed, burdened—and even had some self-pity![15]

Even someone like Lin, who many minorities look up to, struggled with self-absorption. Some of this, we must remember, also came from years of facing similar pressures in high school and college—where he was also regularly taunted with racial slurs. But Lin shared in the interview how over time he came to appreciate the unique opportunity he had to do good for the Asian American community. With strong support from family, friends, and his personal faith, Lin began to embrace and even love the platform and voice he had. Lin said, "It is not a burden to me anymore. I am not scared anymore. I appreciate it and want to help and challenge the world, stereotypes and everything. Back then, I didn't understand it; and it came so fast, I didn't really know what was going on."[16]

It took time and patience for Lin to build up his capacity to see and serve others, but now he is a confident spokesperson about race and faith-related issues in professional sports—even discussing the relationship between African American and Asian American cultures and communities.[17]

Sometimes we can become impatient with ourselves and other people as we navigate our journeys of racial identity. For a while, I was very hard on myself for not seeing the pain of the African American, Latino, and Native American communities around me. I judged people around me who "didn't get it." However, I soon realized that this approach was not helpful, as it made me isolate myself in shame, and took me away from interaction and community.

In 2017, I was asked to lead a multicultural seminar at a Cru leadership gathering. I knew I didn't have all the answers, so I first asked my Latino coworker and friend Daniel to colead the seminar. Then we reached out and asked leaders in various Cru minority groups to share their best insights at our seminar. I learned so much in the process, and am still learning every day. My painful journey of racial identity has shown me how much I don't understand, but I am now more patient with myself than I was before.

Finally, we don't have to look or go far to see minorities who are invisible, or people who are in pain. In fact, there's a good chance they are in your very office, church, or neighborhood grocery store.

One of the most polarizing topics in the United States today is immigration, especially as it pertains to Latinos who cross the Mexican border from the south. Many fear that those who are not legal citizens of the United States will take American jobs away, or increase crime or drugs coming across the border. However, I've come to see the history behind why this topic is so emotionally charged for Latinos, as it surfaces the invisibility and injustice they have experienced for centuries.[18] In too many immigration debates, we overlook the factors of pain, power, and the past.

In his acclaimed book *Harvest of Empire*, Juan Gonzalez suggests that immense Latino immigration and population growth is the direct result of the United States' economic and political involvement (or interference) with Latin American countries.

Many of today's Southwestern states were previously the property of Spanish settlers and eventually the Mexican government, after Mexico declared its independence from Spain in 1821.[19] When white settlers spread into these regions and built plantations, they drove Mexican peasants from their lands. The American government annexed these territories through political manipulation and military force, coercing Mexico through the Treaty of Guadalupe Hidalgo to accept the Rio Grande as the southern border of the United States.[20]

As a result, millions of Mexicans did not even move an inch, but because of the treaty were suddenly considered foreigners in the very land they had owned. While some stayed, others moved south to flee discrimination from white settlers, or to simply live under their own government and laws. Thus, the history of Mexico is embedded with injustice, as many Latinos were driven from their original homes.

Gonzalez goes on to describe how in the centuries since the Treaty of Guadalupe Hidalgo, the United States has been incredibly involved in the political and economic affairs of Latin American countries, including Guatemala, Cuba, Chile, Peru, Nicaragua, Grenada, and Panama, through, for example, regime changes and business deals. Some of this was because of the profitability of investing in mining, petroleum, and manufacturing. Some of this was because Latin America became a chessboard for military maneuvers between the United States and Russia during the Cold War (hence the Cuban Missile Crisis of 1962).

This incessant overinvolvement in Latin America was the direct cause of poverty among peasants in these countries. These peasants were then forced to look north for employment, and were often recruited for cheap labor among white business owners![21]

In summary, many Latinos come to the United States because of conditions that have roots in North American business and politics. The Latino minority experience is that whites interfered with their economy, independence, and way of life. Then after whites recruited them across the border for cheap labor, they shut the door and said, "You're not welcome anymore."[22]

Many Latino minorities experience the message of "We need you, but we don't want you." Jim Wallis describes this as the experience of feeling trapped between two signs: "No Trespassing!" and "Help Wanted."[23]

Years ago, I didn't understand the history behind the immigration debate, nor did I recognize that the economies of Latin

America and the United States are so intertwined. However, every so often I notice that the price of strawberries at the local grocery store have skyrocketed, and discover that it's tied to a strike in Mexico. Every day, I'm more aware of ethnic minorities in labor jobs in my work and home community, and wonder about the systemic forces that might have driven them here.

To be clear, Latinos occupy a variety of jobs across the socio-economic spectrum, and there are workers of many ethnicities in the agriculture and service industry. My Chinese grand-mother-in-law farmed the fields of Salinas, California. Regardless of ethnic background, I'm learning just how many "invisible" people are all around me—at my work office, at church, or at the neighborhood restaurant. It's so easy to look past them, isn't it?

"We need you, but we don't want you." That statement is the ultimate form of invisibility for minorities. Ralph Ellison wrote, "I am invisible, understand, simply because people refuse to see me."[24] Many are living among others in plain sight, but aren't truly seen or valued. Today, I try to look these people in their eyes, ask their name, and (when appropriate) thank them for what they are doing. It may not be much to do, but it's a small way that I'm trying to see minorities who were once invisible to me. I recognize that in many ways I am still blind, but I am slowly learning to see—and I only ask for the compassion to continue to see a little more with each new day.

STEWARDING POWER
WITH HANDS OF ADVOCACY

Why do we turn against each other . . . and can we work together?

I felt blindsided.

For the past few months, I had helped to guide and facilitate a significant leadership selection process in Epic and Cru. I had helped to gather input and outline thoughts on a fair process and criteria that considered the voices across the organization.

And all of a sudden, I learned that some of my coworkers had moved forward with a decision without me.

They didn't tell me about it. I stumbled on it when I was reading the written notes from a meeting that I wasn't able to attend.

I felt confused at first, then shocked. And then the more I learned what had happened, I felt betrayed.

Together with a trusted friend who was facilitating this leadership selection process with me, we called a meeting to discuss what happened. I heard apologies, but there were no attempts to revisit the decision and include my input on a second pass.

I didn't get it. If these leaders needed and wanted me to facilitate the entire process, why would they exclude me at the most important point of the decision? I felt used . . . I felt that my efforts and contributions were only to serve their needs and agenda.

I remember punching and kicking the pillows on my couch in anger. Jenny said, "There is so much baloney going on right now. It doesn't matter what kind of work you put into all this—they're just going to do what they're going to do."

A couple weeks later, I set up a one-on-one meeting with one of the leaders to see if I could understand what was happening. By the end of the lunch, I was in tears. I felt in that moment that no matter what I did, my leaders might never truly see and understand me. An emotion of deep sadness came over me.

It hurt all the more, since I was a younger Asian American leader—exactly the kind of person our organization said it valued and wanted to develop.

Why was this happening . . . in my own community?

TALKING ABOUT SABOTAGE

This wasn't the last time I would experience sabotage in the ethnic minority community. In addition, I have heard many stories from my Asian American mentors of the intense competition they had experienced in the past for opportunities to speak and represent their respective ministries. I spoke to a Latino friend who told me how he was intentionally blocked from writing an article by a more senior Latino leader.

Granted, I'm not completely innocent. Have you ever looked at a successful leader and felt envious? Maybe they've gotten to speak at a huge conference and everyone is buzzing about it. Maybe they've written a book or a blog that's gone viral on social media. Maybe they've started a company that's raking in huge paychecks and fame in the newspapers.

I've had this feeling of envy before. And the feeling can be even more intense when it's a minority leader. And then I feel guilty about it—and wonder what's wrong with me.

The more I've reflected on this, it strikes me how I have a stronger reaction when the successful person is similar to me. For instance, I'm an Asian American male who writes and speaks about leadership and race. So if I see another Asian American male writer who is thriving in leadership circles, it causes more of a reaction in me than a famous African American woman would. It's as if a mirror gets turned back to me, and I wonder, "Will anyone ever notice me too? Am I not as valuable as that person is?"

Why does this happen?

I believe it has everything to do with the minority experience. Again, it may not make as much sense until we think about history and the past, and the lack of opportunities for minorities to have their voices and perspectives heard. Every time I walk into a room full of white leaders, I know I have to put on my best face and prove myself, because otherwise I simply may not be seen. I know I come in with a disadvantage.

In this kind of setting, minorities feel the lack of space for our voice. *We fear there won't be enough space for all of us to be heard.* And so there's a natural competition for the few roles we see are available for people like us. We may feel naturally threatened by those who are like us, who we fear may take the space that we desperately want and need for ourselves.

Joy Lentz Wong describes this well in *Mirrored Reflections*, a compilation of articles written by Asian American women leaders. She writes: "[I felt that] there was only room for one at the top, . . . that we were all competing for the same prize. Thus, my position was inversely proportional with the position of others. If they were lifted up, it meant that I was lowered. If they were ahead, it meant that I was behind. I was uncomfortable when others were praised, because it usually meant that they had achieved something that I had not attained."[1]

Daniel Sanchez defines this philosophy of "limited good" as *envidia* for Latinos. According to this mindset, an "individual or family can improve only at the expense of others."[2] Sociologist Christena Cleveland files this under "realistic conflict theory," which describes how conflict naturally develops between groups that are competing for scarce resources.[3]

Those resources might be a leadership title or even a position of influence and esteem. For some minority leaders who have worked a lifetime fighting for their communities, they may have carved out a niche and identity that isn't so easy to give up.

This could be at the heart of why it's so challenging for older generations in minority organizations and churches to transition to the next generation of leaders. This is part of why leadership change is so difficult, emotional, and polarizing. It stirs up questions of identity, value, and worth.

The book *Growing Healthy Asian American Churches* describes this dynamic well. Peter Cha, Paul Kim, and Dihan Lee write about how the younger generation of Asian American leaders grow up asserting their opinions, which sometimes challenge the older generation's traditional value systems and perspectives. This can cause older leaders to react with hurt or alarm, and sometimes dig even "deeper into their traditional mode of thinking and practice. As a result, the generational and cultural gulf between the two generations widens while the tension escalates."[4]

Another reason that may explain the sabotage phenomenon is that *we sometimes perpetuate the trauma that we ourselves have experienced.* We discussed the impact of abusive efforts to domesticate Lakota Walter Littlemoon through white boarding schools, but one consequence of his trauma is a bit surprising. Littlemoon not only felt embarrassed to talk about his culture, but when an elderly Lakota woman approached him, he even told her not to speak the Lakota language.[5] He felt so much shame—accumulated from his own experiences and the traumas of his family and ancestors—that he subconsciously began to perpetuate the domestication process to other ethnic minorities.

I wonder how many ethnic minorities have been tempted to do something similar—to discourage cultural expression in other minorities because of our fear of facing the shameful and embarrassing parts of our own culture?

In *Mending the Divides*, Jon Huckins and Jer Swigart tell the story of Juanita, an undocumented woman who worked until she got accepted into one of the most prestigious art schools in the United States. However, Juanita's own parents then revealed her undocumented status, forcing her to turn down this life-changing offer.[6] Although Juanita went on to become a spokesperson about the challenges of undocumented children, it must have been doubly painful that people from her own family and culture seemed to turn on her.

Her family may have feared the shame that might come on the family or community if the truth about Juanita had come out later into her education. But we also see the same pattern—those who have been overlooked and mistreated often perpetuate this behavior to their own people. I think way back to Moses in Egypt, when he saw two enslaved Israelites fighting each other and asked, "Men, you are brothers; why do you want to hurt each other?" (Acts 7:26).

Sometimes we can also sabotage minorities who are part of a different community. Perhaps one of the most well-known cases of interminority conflict took place during the 1992 Los Angeles riots between the African American and Korean American communities. The riots killed more than fifty people, injured more than one thousand, and caused approximately one billion dollars in damage, about half of which was sustained by Korean-owned businesses.[7]

Like most racial violence, the tension had been building for years, as Korean merchants had begun to enter the same space in South Central Los Angeles, purchasing businesses from white owners who were leaving the neighborhood. Then, on March 16, 1991, Korean store owner Soon Ja Du fatally shot Latasha Harlins, a fifteen-year-old African American girl who Du accused of shoplifting. When Du was convicted of voluntary manslaughter but was immediately given probation after posting a $250,000 bail, it was the powder keg that ignited the explosive violence during the riots—where African American looters specifically targeted Korean merchants and stores.[8]

Again, consider the history of African Americans facing domestication and injustice in their interactions with law enforcement. When they saw another minority seem to echo this pattern of abuse—whether shooting an unarmed black girl or getting released on immediate probation—it caused them to turn on another minority group with whom they had very little history.[9]

WHY DID HEROD AND PILATE BECOME FRIENDS?

One sad impact of the abuse of power is the way it can cause minorities to turn against one another. Sometimes it's easy to forget that this happened to Jesus himself. Throughout his three years of ministry, Jesus was threatened by Jewish religious leaders who plotted on a way to kill him. When Jesus was finally betrayed by one of his own disciples (Judas), he was arrested, taken through an unlawful trial, beaten, taunted, and executed in one of the most shameful public manners—crucifixion.

This is a story that I've read and heard thousands of times, but now that I've studied minority history, I see a couple of elements in Jesus' story that are remarkable.

First, the religious leaders and Roman authorities alike took many actions to "domesticate" Jesus. They tried to manipulate his words to fit their accusations (Luke 22:63–23:3). They led him like an animal down the street, with crowds surrounding to watch (Luke 23:26-27).[10] There is much about crucifixion that is strikingly similar to the dehumanizing practice of lynching, which James Cone details in many ways in *The Cross and the Lynching Tree*.

Second, Jewish leaders had been oppressed for years by the Romans, and many of their people longed for a Messiah to fight and bring them their freedom and regain their country. However, the Jewish religious leaders, government, and crowds seemed delighted to execute one of their own people, who many had hoped might be this Messiah. This is the epitome of sabotage—and some might even say self-sabotage. There is a small detail in Luke's Gospel that recounts how Roman governor Pontius Pilate sent Jesus to King Herod, who had felt threatened by Jesus for decades. After Herod questioned Jesus and sent him back to Pilate, Luke's account describes how "that day Herod and Pilate became friends—before this they had been enemies" (Luke 23:5-12). Herod was so driven to sabotage Jesus that it overpowered his hatred of Pilate. Years of domestication under Roman rule did not cause Herod or Jewish leadership to defend Jesus, but rather to turn on one of their own.

Fortunately, this is not the end of the story as Christians know it. Jesus was resurrected three days after his death, and we believe that this was part of Jesus' purpose and plan. The ultimate counter to the experience of sabotage and domestication is advocacy. Jesus did not react to all the taunts and accusations, but instead asked God to forgive those who put him to death (Luke 23:34). He offered salvation to a criminal who was crucified on a cross next to him (Luke 23:40-43).

As Christians, we believe that Jesus sacrificed his life in order to offer forgiveness to humankind. The ancient Jewish system of sacrificing animals to God was built on the premise that there is a cost to any forgiveness of wrongdoing. When we hurt someone we love, and they forgive us, it's not cheap. They have to absorb the impact of what we did to hurt them in order to heal their relationship with us. This is what Jesus did—absorb the impact of the guilt and wrongs of the world. Instead of turning on those who killed him, Jesus advocated for them. The Bible says that he is our advocate with God the Father and "the atoning sacrifice for our sins, and not only for ours but also for the sins of the whole world" (1 John 2:1-2).

When we are the beneficiaries of advocacy, it can free us from the bondage of the cycle by which we perpetuate domestication and abuse to others. The apostle Paul writes, "If God is for us, who can be against us?" (Romans 8:31) and reminds us how Jesus is our advocate who is always interceding on our behalf (Romans 8:34). Even in the face of persecution and those who are considered "as sheep to be slaughtered"—language that echoes of domestication and references the oppression of minority Jews (Psalm 44)—Paul concludes that we are "more than conquerors" and that nothing in creation can separate us from the love of God (Romans 8:37-39).

This incredible truth of God's love overpowering the most evil abuses we might encounter is what has given many minorities throughout history courage and hope. Cone writes about how it was meaningful to black Christians who faced the threat of lynching to know that "Jesus went through an experience of suffering in a manner similar to theirs" and that "faith was the one thing white people could not control or take away."[11]

As minorities, we can know that Jesus not only saw and advocated for the oppressed minorities of his day, but that he endured much of the minority experience himself. When we ourselves experience advocacy, how does this help us to work in solidarity with those in our own communities? What might some examples of inter- and intraminority advocacy look like?

ADVOCATING FOR ONE ANOTHER

On the twenty-fifth anniversary of the Los Angeles riots, about one hundred city officials and members of the African American and Korean American communities gathered at First African Methodist Episcopal Church—home of the oldest black congregation in the city. In the first gathering between the two communities to commemorate the riots, leaders acknowledged the pains of the past and how much work still needed to be done.

Los Angeles city councilman David Ryu shared about his working relationship with African American and former Crips gang member Nathan Redfern, and how they have worked together in the two decades since the riots at a Koreatown nonprofit's dispute resolution center: "Ryu recalled how the two men would go out to businesses in East and South L.A. to help resolve conflicts between Korean store owners and their customers, defusing the types of tense situations that led to the riots."[12]

After a joint choir performance of Korean, black, and Latino groups, there was a time for prayer, and then everyone made their way inside the church to "break bread" (take communion) together. This event was organized by the Korean Churches for Community Development organization, and is an example of what interminority advocacy might look like.

More recent examples include the support from Latino and Asian American leaders for the Black Lives Matter movement.[13] A crowdsourced letter among Asian Americans, designed so that younger minorities can explain to their parents or relatives why they support this issue, has been translated into nearly a dozen languages. One excerpt reads, "In fighting for their own rights, Black activists have led the movement for opportunities not just for themselves, but for us as well. Black people have been beaten, jailed, even killed fighting for many of the rights that Asian Americans enjoy today. We owe them so much in return. We are all fighting against the same unfair system that prefers we compete against each other."[14]

Jose Antonio Vargas, a prominent Filipino activist, said that all minority communities must think about what they can do to support the Black Lives Matter movement. He said, "So much of this country's racial conversation has been very Black and White. The country is now more Asian, more Latino, more mixed-race, and we all have roles to play."[15]

When people of color bring their voices together, it helps grow the sense of common good and flourishing for all that God intended.[16] A few examples that have inspired me follow.

Family advocacy. Actress Meghan Markle caused a huge stir when she became the first American to be engaged to a member of the British royal family since 1939, when King Edward VIII was forced to abdicate due to the controversy.[17] Even more significant, perhaps, is that Markle is biracial (black and white), and she wrote about her realities encountering racism—including people calling her mother the N-word and a "nanny" because she was black in a mostly white neighborhood. However, one of the most striking stories that Markle tells is how her white father bought two sets of dolls—one black and one white—in order to construct a mixed set for her to play with. In a move that echoes back to the Clark doll experiments, Markle's father did not succumb to a fatalistic attitude but sought to give his daughter as many examples of dignity and value as he could. This story illustrates how we don't have to perpetuate domesticating stereotypes in our families.[18]

Intergenerational advocacy. In *Growing Healthy Asian American Churches*, Helen Lee gives examples of how Open Door Presbyterian Church in Virginia has tried to work through the intergenerational issues. They've intentionally set up cross-generational times of relationship building, when the older and younger Asian Americans can get to know each other. They've committed to do the hard work of openly and honestly addressing the challenges and fears they face working together.

In the church context, they also host bilingual services; to them, it's worth sacrificing efficiency and time in order to honor one another in this way. They find ways that each ministry and group can serve one another and their events. Finally, Lee preaches patience and letting this process develop over time.

These ideas can be applied to many contexts where there is potential competition and sabotage among minorities. Behind these ideas is a heart of willingness to give away power and control, when it is often uncomfortable and disorienting to do so. Cha, Kim, and Lee write,

> In the Asian immigrant church context this means that the first-generation leadership does not insist on exercising the power that their traditional culture grants them. Rather, they choose to make room for their young people, inviting them to grow into leadership roles. This also means that second-generation young people, in turn, should respond by honoring their elders, thus setting up an ongoing cycle of mutuality and reciprocity between the two groups.[19]

Paul Tokunaga's Daniel Project is another example of a current successful intergenerational advocacy effort. As a leadership cohort, the Daniel Project provides peers and mentors with whom minorities can bond and grow. It created a camaraderie that continues to this day, as many program alumni continue to meet on their own for encouragement and support.[20] Cohorts like this also serve to counter the temptation to "compete," and grow the overall resources of the minority leadership community—so that there is less burden on any one person to represent their entire ethnic community or organization.

That is the key: when we build the minority leadership community by advocating for one another instead of looking to secure our own safety and significance, we address a root cause of the problem. *When together we create more opportunities for minorities, there is more room for everyone, and less need to compete.* In addition, through advocacy we heal some of our wounds from not feeling heard or valued for who we are. Tokunaga is an example of a minority leader who has used his platform and power to build other leaders, instead of keeping them for himself.

Of course, the healing of wounds in community takes time. Because of his abusive experiences of attempted domestication, Walter Littlemoon struggled to find beauty and good in his own Lakota heritage, and was even tempted to sabotage his own people. However, over the next thirty years through counseling and healing in community, Littlemoon learned to separate the negative messages from his past from the positive memories— and to find peace in who he was. In a powerful vision one day, he saw rich memories of his Lakota friends Good Lance, dressed in a purple silk shirt, and Tall Jenny, wearing her scarf and friendly smile. He heard the advice of his childhood mentors with renewed clarity.[21] Instead of perpetuating the domestication process within his own community, Littlemoon saw the beauty of the Lakota people as they were, and this drove his process to share his experiences through his book. It took three decades, but Littlemoon transformed his painful past into advocacy for his people.

STICKING AROUND

Finally, there is my own story of how I learned to work through the tensions and challenges within my own ethnic minority community. In 2016, when I chose to step down from leading Epic's Leadership Development team, I wrestled with what to do. I didn't want to leave the team, and yet what role would I play if I were to stick around? Would I get in the way of the next round of leaders, and how would they be impacted by my presence? I had plenty of doubts, questions, and insecurities—and I understood why so many leaders move on to other teams and organizations when they leave leadership positions.

In the end, I decided to stay on the team in a supportive role. I reduced my hours on the team, but made myself available as a consultant and support to our new team leader, TJ. With her guidance, I continued to create resources to cultivate leadership in the ministry.

There were certainly some moments when I felt some doubt and discomfort. Sometimes I struggled to step back from responsibilities and roles that were no longer mine. Other times I hesitated to appropriately step forward when I had something unique to offer. There were moments when I wondered whether the team and organization were moving on, and I wasn't sure how important or needed I was anymore.

At the same time, I found myself enjoying seeing younger leaders—including T. J.—step up and grow in confidence. I was refreshed hearing their new voices and perspectives that represent a changing world. I learned a lot from the younger leaders on that team. It wasn't without discomfort, but it was rewarding in a way I couldn't have imagined, had I continued up the ladder of positional leadership and promotion.

Also, my new role allowed me the time and space not only to begin writing about my experiences as a minority in Cru, but to circle back on some of my more painful experiences. Earlier, I mentioned interviewing Tommy Dyo, who was executive director of Epic during the time I experienced my biggest leadership challenges. During our lunch, I decided to talk with him about these moments when I felt unseen and blindsided.

Tommy acknowledged where he had missed and made mistakes, and I admitted where I could have been clearer about what I needed from him and his leadership team. He thanked me for circling back with him, and offered his full support for my future endeavors. It wasn't an easy conversation, and it was emotional for both of us. We talked honestly about the challenges of confrontation and vulnerability within the Asian American community.

However, as Tommy and I finished our lunch that weekday afternoon, I felt grateful that we were talking. In past decades, I had avoided too many of these conversations, and I was reminded that it's never too late to circle back on our experiences of pain from the past. I thought not only about Tommy, but about my conversation with Richard. As we face the good and difficult parts of our history, how might we grow and heal? Even more, who knows what advocates we might gain along the way?

REFRAMING THE PAST
WITH A HEART OF WISDOM

Are differences a curse or a blessing?

In 2016, *Washington Post* writer Eli Saslow wrote an article
called "The White Flight of Derek Black" that earned a finalist
spot in the Pulitzer Prize awards for journalism.[1] Saslow details
the remarkable transformation story of Black, the son of former
Ku Klux Klan leader Don Black and godson of white supremacist politician David Duke. At age ten, Derek built the children's page for a white nationalist website called Stormfront
that attracted more than three hundred thousand users. At age
nineteen, he was hosting a daily radio show to share his views
about how whites were losing their culture and traditions to a
massive influx of non-white immigration.

Derek's father and many white nationalists saw Derek as the
future hope of their movement, and believed he could infiltrate
the world of politics to take power back for whites. Could anything stop the passing of racist ideology from one generation to

the next? Was Derek doomed to repeat and continue the events and attitudes of the past?

As it turned out, Derek enrolled in a liberal arts college to study European (white) history, and began to build relationships with people of very different races and backgrounds. His views slowly began to broaden, even as he discreetly continued to host his radio show about the problem of "white genocide." Then someone at Derek's college discovered his connections with white supremacists, and his friends felt betrayed but wondered how the guy they had come to know and like could have such radical associations.

Though Derek moved off campus to avoid the public shame that was thrown his way, one of his Jewish friends invited him to a weekly Shabbat dinner where people discussed culture, religion, and a myriad of other topics. Over time, Derek found himself learning much about the blacks, Latinos, and other minorities who came to these dinners—and gradually found himself changing his views. Eventually, Derek publically wrote about his disaffiliation from white nationalism. This was hard for many in his family and previous community to accept, particularly his father. Don Black considered his son's actions a betrayal. Most people in the white nationalism movement no longer speak with Derek.

This powerful article details the difficulty of confronting the past, with all its expectations that future generations carry forward its assumptions and beliefs. For many whites and minorities throughout history, there's a question of whether or not we can ever get out of the cycles of crosscultural tension and hate. Derek Black's story shows that it is possible, especially through the care that his college friends showed for him when others had shamed and alienated him. However, crosscultural relationships and understanding are painful, and come at a cost.

OUR SHARED HISTORY OF PAIN

It is an inescapable reality that whites and minorities have a shared history that contains much violence and pain. As I've studied the history of the United States, it has struck me how each minority group's story follows the same pattern: (1) they sought the same jobs as white workers, (2) employers used their power over minorities to get them to accept lower wages (or even forced labor), and (3) white workers resented minorities for "taking away" their jobs—resulting in violence.[2] It was clear to see this with whites and Chinese,[3] Mexicans,[4] South Asians,[5] Filipinos,[6] Vietnamese,[7] Haitians, Cubans, and countless other minority communities.[8]

This pattern has existed since the eighteenth century—when white employers first turned to African slave labor to avoid confrontation with the white working class (e.g., Bacon's Rebellion[9]). Is it any wonder that the successful presidential campaign of 2016 was based on tapping into this fear that the United States may be losing its jobs and ways to those on the "outside"? It was incredibly effective because these fears and competitive forces have existed for centuries.

What has been the impact of the past on the psychological and emotional realities of minorities, and the majority culture?

For minorities, there are a variety of ways that history has shaped our response to the majority culture. In 2014, I wrote a Cru article with my African American, Latino, and Native American coworkers called "Six Postures of Ethnic Minority Culture Towards Majority Culture."[10] We identified six different "postures" that minorities might take toward whites:

1. *Unaware.* This means that we may either be unconscious about our racial differences or choose not to talk about them.

2. *Angry and Wounded.* We may feel anger because of the injustices and betrayals of history, or due to racism that we have experienced.

3. *Silent and Resigned.* At times we can internalize our pain and feel there is nothing we can do to change our reality.

4. *Duty and Pleasing.* We may be so used to being under the power of whites that we act in a subservient manner, needing approval or permission before choosing to talk or act.

5. *Unity as Assimilation.* Sometimes in the desire to seek "unity," we might discard important elements of our distinctiveness as minorities. What looks like unity is actually uniformity.

6. *Equal and Empowered.* This means that we see ourselves as equally valuable as whites, and as a result build crosscultural partnerships for both sides' benefit. We take the

initiative out of the beauty of how God created us, rather than out of reaction to how others try to define us.

Many people have told us that they found this framework, and its predecessor "Five Majority Culture Postures Toward Ethnic Minority Ministry,"[11] helpful—and both articles are part of Cru's training curriculum that every staff takes. In my cross-cultural experiences, I found myself navigating between two extreme options: *Do I assimilate, or do I disengage?*

For instance, in Epic I worked on a team that was half white and half minority. Sometimes I found it difficult to challenge the opinions of the white men because I wanted to fit in. I remember another time when I was hurt by a comment my white teammate said, and my instinct was to shut down and withdraw. When we talked about it later, I was surprised to find myself in tears, feeling an intensity and depth of emotion that I didn't expect. Over time, I began to see that my past experiences of working hard to be accepted—along with my experiences of rejection and racism— had made me weary.

For minorities, what might seem like a small incident is never disconnected from the past. An African American inner-city resident put it well: "You try so hard it seems as if when you just about to get up, something happen to knock you back down and you just forget it, then."[12] The minority experience is not a series of unrelated events on a timeline. It is more like a cumulative painting of emotions and experiences on a canvas. It builds and can wear minorities down.

How does the past affect members of the majority culture? In *White Awake*, Daniel Hill describes the concept of *white trauma* outlined by Navajo activist Mark Charles.[13] This is the observation that when a majority group has a history tainted with abuse, such as that of white settlers taking over Native American lands, it cannot help but dehumanize and traumatize the oppressors as well. Indeed, many whites feel shame and struggle with how to engage conversations about race and diversity. Some try to disassociate with whiteness completely, and sometimes they choose to identify instead with minority cultures.

Others may react with defensiveness or anger. Some whites may seek to avoid talking about race at all and isolate themselves—a sign of what Robin DiAngelo calls *white fragility*, or low stamina when it comes to engaging crosscultural stress.[14]

Although there are huge disparities in pain and power between majority and minority cultures, the behavior of both groups have certain similarities. It is easy for both groups—when faced with crosscultural stress and the trauma of the past—to "deny" who they are, disengage from each other, or both.

The biggest challenge is to first accept who we are, in all the good and bad of that—without rejecting, denying, or minimizing any of it. Then the next step is to still engage each other across the gap of pain, power, and the past. Is this possible?

I ONCE WAS SAUL

The very origins of Christianity may provide an example. After all, Christianity began as a sect of Judaism known simply as

"The Way," and Jesus' first followers operated as a minority group within the Jewish community. In the first years of Christian ministry, Saul was a zealous Jew (part of a group called the Pharisees) who persecuted and killed Christians. However, one day while traveling on a road to the city of Damascus, Saul had a religious experience in which Jesus appeared to him in a vision. Jesus confronted Saul and charged him to stop killing Christians and instead help spread the message of Christianity to both Jews and non-Jews (Acts 9:1-16).

This is not only one of the most dramatic conversion stories in the Bible, but it resulted in a radical shift from Christianity being only a small Jewish sect to spreading to all non-Jewish (called "Gentiles" in the Bible) people groups throughout the world. The newly appointed apostle Paul traveled throughout Asia, Europe, and Africa to share the message of Jesus, and mentored churches and bicultural leaders like Timothy along the way. Thus, the spread of Christianity happened through the opening of one ethnic group to many other communities.

This process was not without conflict, as many Jewish leaders did not feel comfortable with these changes. Paul had to confront one of Jesus' disciples, Peter, about his fear of being judged for associating with Gentiles (Galatians 2:11-14). Throughout his ministry, Paul was threatened and attacked by Jewish leaders who felt he was turning their people against their culture and religion (Acts 21:27-36; 23:1-22; 24:1-27). In each case, it would have been easy for Paul to disassociate himself from his Pharisee past, due to shame for his previous persecution of Christians.

Instead, Paul clearly owned that he was a Jew and Pharisee (Acts 21:39; 23:6; 26:4-5), and admitted his wrongdoings against Christianity. He also claimed that it was because of his belief in God's promises to the Jews that he followed Jesus (Acts 22:4-16; 24:14-16; 26:6-23). While on trial in Caesarea, he reminded the governor Felix that he believed "everything that is in accordance with the Law and that is written in the Prophets," and that compelled him to believe in the resurrection and message of Jesus (Acts 24:14-16). Paul was able to acknowledge the bad parts of his cultural past, such as the abuse and injustices he committed. However, he didn't renounce that part of his identity, but owned it and claimed that Jesus provided an even better fulfillment of what his Jewish ancestors longed for.

Paul is a remarkable example of someone who did not deny his identity and history, nor disengage with those who were different from him. He acknowledged the past, but did not let it paralyze him into a fatalistic mentality. Of course, it was no accident that this happened, as God in his wisdom does not see history as random but purposeful—and he used Paul's past in a redemptive way. Sarah Shin puts it well:

> Before his encounter with Christ, Paul represented a broken, oppressed people full of resentment toward every ethnicity that was not their own. But now his mission was to reach all, which meant crossing cultures, reconciling

with ethnic enemies, caring for the poor, confronting injustice, and proclaiming Jesus as Lord. New life in Jesus brought healing to Paul's ethnic identity. Jesus took all of Paul's great knowledge and zeal for the Jewish Scriptures and turned that ethnic story into one that invited all into the kingdom of God.[15]

EXAMPLES OF PARTNERSHIP

Of course, we cannot always see God's bigger purpose for history. However, we can control our own actions and choices. The choice in front of all of us is clear—to not deny who we are, but to continue to engage those who are different from us.

What can this look like? Much talk about crosscultural work is often labeled "racial reconciliation," and focuses on how to have healthy and constructive partnerships across majority and minority culture lines.[16] However, Brenda Salter McNeil defines reconciliation much more broadly: "Reconciliation is an ongoing spiritual process involving forgiveness, repentance, and justice that restores broken relationships and systems to reflect God's original intention for all creation to flourish."[17] To McNeil, reconciliation means not just human-to-human relationships, but the healing of unjust systems of society and the world. The following examples should illustrate this.

Bruce Lee and Linda Emery. "What? I'm related to Bruce Lee?" I remember my incredulous response to my mother, who showed me the family tree that connects the actor and *Jeet Kune Do* legend to us. Suddenly, the "all Asians know martial arts" jokes people had thrown my way took on a new irony. As I began to study Lee's life in more depth, I discovered how much of a crosscultural trailblazer he was. While Lee faced a lot of racism, he persisted in wanting to teach his culture and arts to whites and non-Chinese—for which he faced disapproval from the Asian community. Lee's first student was an African American man, Jesse Glover, who he trained to be a teacher. Finally, he married a white woman, Linda Emery. Together, Bruce and Linda Lee spread Chinese culture and martial arts around the country and world. Linda wrote,

> The big issue [with our relationship] was the interracial aspect. [My family] felt we would suffer the slings and arrows of society's prejudice, and our children likewise. My aunt and uncle were very religious and they thought the mixing of the races was an abomination. On the contrary, I felt strongly that God would bless our union.[18]

Despite facing opposition from both white and minority communities, the Lees didn't deny who they were, nor stop engaging either group.

Highway 93 in Montana. There are countless stories of tension between white efforts to expand technology or infrastructure, and Native resistance because of the way these expansions will impact their lands, sacred traditions, and the health of the environment. In 2016, much national attention was brought to the Dakota Access Pipeline, a 1,200-mile-long project designed to transport barrels of crude oil daily from North Dakota to Illinois. Many celebrities traveled to join protests originated by the Standing Rock Sioux tribe, who are concerned that a leak may damage the tribe's water supply, and also argue that the pipeline traverses a sacred burial ground. While pipeline supporters point out that the project is not technically on the tribe's reservation, the Standing Rock Sioux argue that the United States government did not adequately engage their tribe during the permitting process. One can see the impact of the past on the tensions of this debate.[19]

In contrast, one example of a successful partnership that seeks to respect Native lands, traditions, and the environment is Highway 93 in Montana. Randy Woodley describes this road as the first to include passes for wildlife to go over and under the roads.[20] More and more, Woodley hears of churches involving Native Americans as consultants to help them understand the relationship between God and the environment, and this is an example of a partnership that can fix broken systems of the past.

Minority leaders leading all races. Woodley also writes about a Native church where whites decided to give up their positions of power to Native Americans. This had a much greater impact than simply incorporating certain instruments or rituals in the service.[21] Indeed, I attribute much of the success of Epic Movement, growing from twenty to over one hundred staff, to the freedom that we as minorities had to lead the organization, including white staff. This required the humility of white coworkers who had more racial and organizational power to accept positions under minority leadership.[22]

This is an exciting reality of the world we now live in where more minorities are in visible leadership positions—and this is not just "cosmetic diversity," these leaders truly grasp the depth of what it means to be a minority! Examples include Tom Lin (president of InterVarsity Christian Fellowship), Nikki Toyama-Szeto (executive director of Evangelicals for Social Action), Noel Castellanos (president of CCDA), Leroy Barber (executive director of the Voices Project), Jenny Yang (vice president of World Relief), and Jemar Tisby (president of The Witness: A Black Christian Collective).

There are activists such as Lisa Sharon Harper, Alexia Salvatierra, Mark Charles, Kathy Khang, and Sandra Van Opstal. There are professors such as Soong-Chan Rah, Daniel White Hodge, Randy Woodley, Robert Chao Romero, Kay Higuera Smith, Daniel Carroll, and the late Richard Twiss. I could list many others, but there are many opportunities for minorities to lead in ways that didn't exist before!

NOT ALONE

When we reflect on the past as minorities, it can fill us with a sense of weariness as we consider the pain and abuses of power that our ancestors endured. However, we are not doomed to repeat history, and God has not left us alone. I think of Derek Black and his moment of shame when his family and community history of white nationalism were exposed to his friends.

He responded by isolating himself, and struggled to define who he was and what he believed. However, his friends didn't leave him alone, but reached out. Matthew Stevenson, organizer of the Shabbat dinners, decided that "his best chance to affect Derek's thinking was not to ignore him or confront him, but simply to include him." Stevenson instructed the other dinner attendees to "treat him like anyone else."[23] More than intellectual debates and research, I believe this simple act of love at Black's deepest moment of shame may have been the turning point that gave Derek the courage to steer from the trajectory of his white nationalist past.[24]

For majority and minority cultures, our history is inextricably woven together, and there is no escaping this reality. It is *how* we navigate this history, and our differences, that will shape the future.

THE CHALLENGE
AND THE OPPORTUNITY

Often during my decade of full-time work with Cru, people would ask me, "Why do you choose to work for a majority-white organization? Why not move to an organization that has only ethnic minorities?" It is a good question, and I do believe it is healthy for minorities to find support in a community that understands them. But I usually answered, "Because the challenge of Cru is the challenge of America." Indeed, the emotional realities I've described in this book about self-doubt, domestication, weariness, invisibility, sabotage, and crosscultural relationships are not unique to a particular organization. They are simply the realities of the minority experience that come with living in a diverse society.

As long as this world exists, there will always be power disparities among various communities. There will always be a unique pain that comes out of these disparities—often from scars of the past that carry across the memories of many generations.

In his research on high-performing teams and organizations, London Business School professor Randall Peterson concludes that diversity is a double-edged sword—it can result in either the lowest or the highest performance. That is because diversity requires more work and time to bring about cohesion and collaboration, but it also fosters greater breadth of knowledge and creative depth.[1] So what is the one factor that helps an organization or country to avoid the pitfalls of diversity, and steward its strengths to greater heights? Leadership.

The biggest challenge of race, politics, and any polarizing issue in society today is not to determine who is right or wrong. Those debates will likely never end, nor be resolved. More importantly, *how do we engage people who are different from us?* That is the great challenge and opportunity of leadership today. I decided to continue to work part-time with Cru because I embrace this challenge. One reason I choose to live in the United States is that I believe there is value and honor in the quest to work out our differences.

The struggle between majority and minority people groups is not unique to the United States, and it has been long depicted through analogies in fantasy and science fiction genres, such as the X-Men series. I was watching the movie *X-Men: Days of Future Past*, in which a young Charles Xavier sees all the pain of the mutants throughout the world. He becomes overwhelmed by it, and by his anger at those who have caused the pain. He blames humanity (an analogy for the majority culture) for causing mutants (the minorities) all this pain.

In a vision, however, an older, wiser version of Xavier counsels him.

> Old Charles: "[We must] show them a better path. Just because somebody stumbles, loses their way . . . it doesn't mean they're lost forever. Sometimes we all need a little help."
>
> Young Charles: "All those voices. So much pain."
>
> Old Charles: "It's not their pain you're afraid of. It's yours, Charles. And as frightening as it may be, their pain will make you stronger . . . if you allow yourself to feel it.
>
> "Embrace it. It will make you more powerful than you ever imagined. It's the greatest gift we have: to bear their pain without breaking. And it's borne from the most human bond . . . hope.
>
> "Please, Charles . . . we need you to hope again."

To bear their pain without breaking—there is a cost to this that Professor Xavier feels strongly. It even made him want to forsake his mutant powers. However, as he learns to embrace his identity, Xavier stewards his power to ultimately change history and save humanity from destruction.

I see ethnic minorities in a similar light. While we may not have superhuman powers, we possess an incredible power because of our experiences and history. God has given us a vast capacity for compassion because of the pain we and our ancestors have suffered. God has given us the gift of collaboration and advocacy, which allows us to mobilize entire ethnic communities seemingly overnight for social causes. God has given us the wisdom and resilience of our minority pioneers and prophets who were forced to migrate and find new lands.

Adversity builds strength. Earlier, I referred to the *X2: X-Men United* scene where the mutants barely escape as Jean Grey holds back the flooding waters before she is overwhelmed. However, the closing moments of the film show a shining silhouette of a large bird-like figure rising to the surface of the dam waters. In the next movie, we discover that Jean Grey was resurrected to new life in an even stronger form, the Phoenix. As I watched this scene, I couldn't help but think of the spiritual applications.

After all, it wasn't just in a myth or movie that Jesus bore the pain of humanity. It was reality—that he embraced this pain, and transformed it into an opportunity for all to experience forgiveness and new life through his death and resurrection! He has not left us alone, but given us hope—in his ongoing presence, and in his gift of so many of our white and minority coworkers and friends on the journey. They are our *partners in pain*.

In closing, let's recall the reminders to the people of Israel in Deuteronomy:

- Remember how God led you through pain. You endured famine and wandering in the wilderness for forty years, and God used this to humble and teach you. When you are eating food in the comfort of your homes, do not forget it is God who truly satisfies.

- Remember how God led you through power. You were enslaved in Egypt, and God saw you and led you out.

When things are going well, you may say to yourself that "my own power and strength" have produced my wealth. Do not forget that it is God who gives you your abilities.

- Remember how God led you through history. Do not forget that God is faithful and remembers the promises he made to your ancestors. When you become large in number, do not forget that you were once the fewest in number among all peoples.

Finally,

- God does not show partiality, and he defends the cause of the widow and loves the foreigner residing among you. So you too are to love those who are foreigners, for you yourselves were foreigners in Egypt. Do not forget this.

What a perfect reminder to the United States, which is large in power, but was once much smaller in stature. When we consider the scope of world history, nations come and go, and power shifts around. We cannot foresee or control what the future holds on that level. The Israelites couldn't imagine God's plan to bring healing and salvation to the Gentiles—to the entire world. The religious leaders of Jesus' day couldn't imagine his plan of global redemption, beyond their desire for political and military deliverance from Roman oppression. Southern slave owners in the 1800s couldn't imagine the way that African American migration would spread black literature, arts, and music to the northern and western cities. But God knew.

It is easy to become discouraged and weary when we see patterns of history that seem to repeat, no matter how much we learn or educate ourselves and others. When we're stuck in the middle of polarizing debates about a topic like race, it's hard to see an end in sight to these cycles. However, the narrative of the Bible is not circular or directionless—it has a beginning, middle, and end. The message of God is that history is not random, but purposeful, and that he is weaving the events of this world together like a master storyteller.

There is movement and change that we can see. The increasing demographics of ethnic minorities in the United States is an undeniable reality that is already shaping the landscape and future leadership of the country. This is an exciting reality that we can, and must steward! The question is, *how* will we navigate these emotional and communal realities?

We know the end of history described in the Bible—an oft-mentioned "great multitude" in the book of Revelation, where people from "every nation, tribe, people and language" gather to worship God together (Revelation 7:9). These people are not assimilated into a melting pot, but retain the distinctiveness and beauty of their cultures. We know the end of the story, but again, *how* will we get there?

Will we see this path as a burden, or as a gift from God?

We cannot see or control the larger narrative of history, but we can control what each of us does today. We can let our pain build compassion, our power build advocacy, and our past build wisdom.

And above all, we can love the widows, the poor, and the foreigners among us.

Pain, power, and the past—they're not a burden that has to weaken us. They are an incredible gift that will stretch our hearts with more capacity for love and understanding than we ever knew we could have. That is the gift of the minority experience.

ACKNOWLEDGMENTS

This book would not have been possible without all the people who believed in it. Thank you to my editor, Al Hsu, who provided just the right mix of freedom and guidance, and of encouragement and truth. Thank you to my marketing manager, Helen Lee, who was such a generous and strategic advocate, and to the rest of the IVP staff for all the ways you provide a platform for ethnic-minority writers. Thank you to readers who provided feedback on early versions of my manuscript, and to my copyeditor—I learned a lot from you.

Thank you to Rick James and Eric Pederson, who did perhaps more than anyone to advocate for this project in the beginning stages. I won't forget what you did for me. Thank you to Tom Virtue, TJ Poon, Eric Hsu, Paul Sorrentino, John Yoon, Joey Chao, and Stan Lin—your ongoing prayers got me through the hardest times of writing and revisions.

Thank you to Charles Lee and Ideation for all the ways you helped to kick-start me toward my goals and dreams. Thank you to Andy Crouch for your time and encouragement.

Thank you to Paula Fuller, David Bennett, and Paul Park for your generous counsel and connections. Thank you to DJ Chuang, Daniel So, and Malcolm Webber for supporting my writing endeavors. I greatly appreciate your wisdom and friendship.

Thank you to Paul Tokunaga, Daniel Lee, Tommy Dyo, and Brian Virtue for sharing your stories and insights with me for this book. Thank you to Grace Hsiao Hanford for your assistance with book sources early on. Thank you to Karen Virtue, Margaret Yu, and Faye Waidley, who first heard my new staff story in a coffee shop—and asked me to share more.

Thank you to Erick Schenkel, Matt Mikalatos, Keith Johnson, and other Cru leaders who provided valuable feedback. Thank you to the Epic Leadership Development team that allowed me the space to begin my work on this book, and to Christine Lin for your support in the later stages of my writing.

Thank you to my parents, sister, and in-laws for your love and prayers during one of the hardest seasons of my life. Most of all, thank you to my wife, Jenny, who sacrificed more than anyone to support me and this book. Partnering with you is the greatest joy of my life.

STUDY GUIDE

INTRODUCTION

1. What is the difference between race and ethnicity, and why is that important?

2. Dr. Martin Luther King Jr. once said, "It is possible to have a quantitative equality and a qualitative inequality." Do you agree? Have you experienced or seen this yourself? Please explain.

1 SELF-DOUBT: UNDERSTANDING PAIN

1. Did any of the Peis' new staff training experience resonate with you? Have you ever wondered if you "were the problem"? Please explain.

2. What is the difference between guilt and shame according to Brené Brown? Do you agree that one is better than the other?

3. What new insights did you take away from the story of Moses, especially as pertaining to his experience as a minority?

4. Think about individuals with whom you have had cross-cultural tension in the past. Would it be worth pursuing a follow-up conversation with any of them?

2 PAIN, POWER, AND THE PAST: THREE DISTINCTIVES OF THE MINORITY EXPERIENCE

1. What does the phrase "Black Lives Matter" have to do with pain? What are the differences between it and the phrase "All Lives Matter"?

2. What are some examples of white privilege, other than the dominance of the English language throughout the world? List as many as you can think of.

3. Pick a recent controversy in the media related to race, whether in sports or entertainment. How might history explain people's reactions to the topic?

4. In what ways did the Israelites experience being minorities while in Egypt and in the wilderness?

3 DOMESTICATION: UNDERSTANDING POWER

1. What is your cultural story? Where did you grow up? What is your parents' or ancestors' immigration story?

2. Name a time you wrestled with trying to change yourself in order to be accepted.

3. What is the difference between prejudice and racism, and why is this important?

4. What new insights did you take away from the story of Daniel, especially as pertaining to his experience as a minority?

4 WEARINESS: UNDERSTANDING THE PAST

1. When you're in a group meeting, do you tend to assert yourself or wait for your turn to speak? Why do you think you have that tendency?

2. Think of ethnic minority friends who have left the group or organization you're in. What were their reasons for leaving, and what did they need?

3. What new insights did you take away from the story of Esther, especially as pertaining to her experience as a minority?

4. Name some movies or television shows that are analogies for minority groups in a dominant culture. What helps those groups to survive?

5 CHALLENGES IN ORGANIZATIONAL DEVELOPMENT: HOW TO DIVERSIFY YOUR ORGANIZATION

1. See the questions within this chapter for discussion in your group.

6 SEEING PAIN WITH EYES OF COMPASSION

1. What are some historic events that were you taught with a positive spin (e.g., Christopher Columbus)?

2. Why is colorblindness not a neutral stance on race?

3. What new insights did you take away from the story of Ruth, especially as pertaining to her experience as a minority?

4. Who are the people around you that are easiest for you to not see? Why?

7 STEWARDING POWER WITH HANDS OF ADVOCACY

1. On a scale from one to ten, how competitive would you say you are? What do you think has made you that way?

2. Have you ever experienced or seen sabotage within the ethnic minority community? What was the impact on the community and on you?

3. What new insights did you take away from the story of Jesus, especially as pertaining to his experience as a minority?

4. Name some examples of minorities you know who have advocated for one another (or for you). How has this been significant for you?

8 REFRAMING THE PAST WITH A HEART OF WISDOM

1. What were the biggest factors that contributed to Derek Black's transformation?

2. Out of all the six postures listed, which one do you currently identify with the most?

3. What new insights did you take away from the story of Paul, especially as pertaining to his crosscultural posture and role?

4. What examples do you know of fruitful crosscultural partnerships? What makes them work?

9 THE CHALLENGE AND THE OPPORTUNITY

1. What are your major takeaways from this book?

2. What have you learned about yourself (and others) while reading this book?

3. What kind of changes are you considering making—personal and organizational—after reading this book?

NOTES

PREFACE

1 Out of the *New York Times'* top five most commented articles of 2017, three are race-related—and have shattered the website's previous records for comments. Marie Tae McDermott, "Trump, Leakers, Travel Ban: Our Most Commented-On Articles of 2017," December 20, 2017, www.nytimes .com/2017/12/20/insider/our-most-commented-on-articles-of-2017.html.

2 I've come to believe there is no perfect approach to the topic of race, since each person is in a different place in his or her own journey. In the debate on race, there will always be some who feel minorities are overfocused on struggles and the past, and have a "victim" mindset. On the other hand, there will always be some who feel that any talk of hope or "solutions" minimizes the pain and struggles of minorities. My goal is not to satisfy everyone, but rather to represent a variety of ideas and approaches, in order to stimulate learning as we each navigate our own journeys.

3 Professor Soong-Chan Rah writes that "storytelling is the ultimate self-disclosure. It reveals insights into the personality, emotions, content, and identity of the individual." This is my personal story, not a detached analysis from an ivory tower. While I do lean heavily on research, I believe some progress can be made as minorities share vulnerably about their experiences with emotional and psychological (rather than just cognitive) language. Soong-Chan Rah, *Many Colors: Cultural Intelligence for a Changing Church* (Chicago: Moody Publishers, 2010), 136.

4 Leah Gunning Francis, *Ferguson & Faith: Sparking Leadership & Awakening Community* (Danvers, MA: Chalice Press, 2015), 112.

5 I recognize that different categories present different challenges, and some applications cannot be made from one category to another.

●INTRODUCTION

[1]Justin Worland, "What to Know About the Dakota Access Pipeline Protests," *Time*, October 28, 2016, http://time.com/4548566/dakota-access -pipeline-standing-rock-sioux.

[2]Beverly Daniel Tatum, *"Why Are All the Black Kids Sitting Together in the Cafeteria?" And Other Conversations About Race* (New York: Basic Books, 1997), 17.

[3]Michael O. Emerson and Christian Smith, *Divided By Faith: Evangelical Religion and the Problem of Race in America* (New York: Oxford University Press, 2000), 7-8.

[4]Lisa Sharon Harper, *The Very Good Gospel: How Everything Wrong Can Be Made Right* (New York: WaterBrook, 2016), 147-48. Drew Hart also mentions that *The Color of Wealth* details more examples of non-whites who went to court seeking to be classified as white in *Trouble I've Seen: Changing the Way the Church Views Racism* (Harrisonburg, VA: Herald Press, 2016), 102. Using race as social power is not new in the scope of history. Harper writes about how Plato's *Republic* attempted to classify people into a hierarchy by "racial" categories represented by various precious metals, which would determine societal status. In 1767, Swedish botanist Carl Linnaeus defined the first taxonomy of human racial hierarchy based on skin color. Harper, *The Very Good Gospel*, 146-47. Race has historically functioned as a way to classify people based on physical characteristics, which are then linked to assumptions about moral or intellectual character.

[5]Dr. Russell Jeung writes about his experiences living among poor Asian Americans in Oakland and how this helped him to see the "pernicious effects of structural injustice and inequities on their lives." Russell Jeung, *At Home in Exile: Finding Jesus Among My Ancestors & Refugee Neighbors* (Grand Rapids: Zondervan, 2016), 50.

[6]Such was the lesson for the late Richard Twiss, who discovered in his work with Native Americans many striking parallels with the challenges of indigenous peoples from around the world, including New Zealand, Australia, Peru, Argentina, South Africa, Samoa, Mexico, Hawaii, Rwanda, Micronesia, Mongolia, and Korea. Richard Twiss, *Rescuing the Gospel from the Cowboys: A Native American Expression of the Jesus Way* (Downers Grove, IL: InterVarsity Press, 2015), 28.

[7] I am Chinese American, but my father grew up in Japan and my mother grew up in Vietnam and speaks seven languages. I lived in three continents by the time I was five years old, so I feel very interconnected with diverse experiences and cultures.

[8] Soong-Chan Rah, *Many Colors: Cultural Intelligence for a Changing Church* (Chicago: Moody Publishers, 2010), 38.

[9] Some may tend to conflate culture with worldview. In Cru's new Intro to Mission class, Dr. Miriam Adeney breaks down culture into three categories: social-relational patterns, material-economic patterns, and worldview. In *Cultural Intelligence*, David Livermore describes culture as *air*—it is invisible, but has a constant presence and influence on everything we do. These terms are not abstract concepts that only apply to some scholars; we live these realities every day. David A. Livermore, *Cultural Intelligence: Improving Your CQ to Engage Our Multicultural World* (Grand Rapids: Baker Academic, 2009), 80-81.

[10] Jim Wallis writes, "Here is the truth: most white people—the vast majority in both the South and the North, including our 'founding fathers'—accepted slavery. Most white people, white Christians, and white churches tolerated slavery in North America for 246 years, from 1619 to 1865." Jim Wallis, *America's Original Sin: Racism, White Privilege, and the Bridge to a New America* (Grand Rapids: Brazos Press, 2016), 37.

[11] When two people or groups are entrenched in a destructive cycle, it often takes a third party to intervene before anything can change. That is why so many couples seek marriage therapy, or why business partners seek mediators or consultants. In his book *Integrity*, leadership expert Dr. Henry Cloud explains this principle by the second law of thermodynamics. Any system tends toward stagnation until there is an injection of life from the outside. I believe that Christianity offers this sort of intervention in God, a higher power who provides a way to break cycles when we learn that we can't with our own strength or willpower. Henry Cloud, *Integrity: The Courage to Meet the Demands of Reality* (New York: HarperCollins, 2006), 220-21.

[12] See Ashley Broughton, "Minorities Expected to Be Majority in 2050," CNN, August 13, 2008, www.cnn.com/2008/US/08/13/census.minorities, and Sam Roberts, "Projections Put Whites in Minority in U.S. by 2050," *New York Times*, December 17, 2009, www.nytimes.com/2009/12/18/us/18census.html.

[13]Although this book will not cover gender issues in depth, applications can be made. Women have historically made up slightly more than 50% of the population of the United States and so are a numerical majority. Still, they have had to fight for equality and voice in the workplace and in society—such as having the right to vote. Women have experienced an imbalance of power in leadership, as there have been to this date 100 percent US male presidents compared to 0 percent female presidents. These are the ways we are viewing what it means to be a minority, not just sheer demographic percentages.

[14]Jeff Chang, *Who We Be: A Cultural History of Race in Post–Civil Rights America* (New York: St. Martin's Press, 2014), 40.

1 SELF-DOUBT

[1]Elizabeth Cohen, "Push to Achieve Tied to Suicide in Asian-American Women," CNN, May 16, 2007, www.cnn.com/2007/HEALTH/05/16/asian.suicides.

[2]Jeff Yang, "Do Asian Students Face Too Much Academic Pressure?," CNN, July 2, 2015, www.cnn.com/2015/07/02/opinions/yang-genius-girl.

[3]Jennifer Chen, "The Dangerous Weight of Expectations," *Pacific Standard*, August 10, 2015, https://psmag.com/the-dangerous-weight-of-expectations-34236d9872b7#.yzuy16hr4.

[4]Brené Brown, "Shame v. Guilt," January 14, 2013, https://brenebrown.com/blog/2013/01/14/shame-v-guilt.

[5]Andy Crouch, "The Return of Shame," *Christianity Today*, March 10, 2015, www.christianitytoday.com/ct/2015/march/andy-crouch-gospel-in-age-of-public-shame.html.

[6]David Brooks, "The Shame Culture," *New York Times*, March 15, 2016, www.nytimes.com/2016/03/15/opinion/the-shame-culture.html?_r=0.

[7]Daniel R. Sanchez, *Hispanic Realities Impacting America: Implications for Evangelism and Missions* (Fort Worth, TX: Church Starting Network, 2006), 104.

[8]Isabel Wilkerson, *The Warmth of Other Suns: The Epic Story of America's Great Migration* (New York: Vintage Books, 2010), 208.

[9]Wilkerson, *Warmth of Other Suns*, 210.

[10]One term well known to ethnic minorities is *liminality*, which means the experience or feeling of being in between two cultures or worlds. For example, Mexican Americans may feel that they don't quite fit in North American culture, but also don't quite fit in Mexican culture. However, liminality is painful for ethnic minorities who didn't voluntarily come to the United States, but were driven from their homes. For Native Americans and many Mexican Americans whose territories were annexed as part of European expansion, white culture was the "second culture" thrust upon them. Lakota author Richard Twiss associates the Native experience of liminality with the loss of their peoples' lands, which had formed their identity. For his people, liminality is an emotional reality of "confusion, loss, fear, the unknown, searching and despair." Richard Twiss, *Rescuing the Gospel from the Cowboys: A Native American Expression of the Jesus Way* (Downers Grove, IL: InterVarsity Press, 2015), 65-66.

[11]Randy Woodley, *Living in Color: Embracing God's Passion for Ethnic Diversity* (Downers Grove, IL: InterVarsity Press, 2001), 54.

[12]A key leader on Cru's theological development team told me that when he heard about Jenny's and my challenging experience at new staff training years ago, it catalyzed his own journey of understanding ethnic minority realities. We never know how sharing our stories might make a difference!

2 PAIN, POWER, AND THE PAST

[1]Fuller Theological Seminary: Asian American Center, http://fuller.edu/asian-american-center.

[2]Dr. Lee's friend Kevin Park, from Columbia Seminary, calls this "ornamental multiculturalism." "Ornamental Multiculturalism and Ecumenism," in *Unity in Mission: Accompanying One Another on the Pilgrimage of Ecumenism*, ed. Mitzi Budde and Don Thorsen (Mahwah, NJ: Paulist Press, 2013).

[3]Sam Cooke, "A Change Is Gonna Come," RCA Victor, December 22, 1964.

[4]Peter Guralnick, *Dream Boogie: The Triumph of Sam Cooke* (New York: Back Bay Books, 2005), 527.

[5]Leah Gunning Francis, *Ferguson & Faith: Sparking Leadership & Awakening Community* (Danvers, MA: Chalice Press, 2015), 82.

[6]Sometimes this comes from a white cultural tendency to emphasize "fairness." See Paula Harris and Doug Schaupp, *Being White: Finding Our Place in a Multiethnic World* (Downers Grove, IL: InterVarsity Press, 2004), 139-40.

[7]Drew Hart, *Trouble I've Seen: Changing the Way the Church Views Racism* (Harrisonburg, VA: Herald Press, 2016), 24-25.

[8]Hart, *Trouble I've Seen*, 26.

[9]Charles Gilmer, *A Cry of Hope, A Call to Action: Unleashing the Next Generation of Black Christian Leaders* (Lake Mary, FL: Creation House, 2009), 29.

[10]Jeanne Wakatsuki Houston and James D. Houston, *Farewell to Manzanar: A True Story of Japanese American Experience During and After the World War II Internment* (New York: Random House, 1973), 7-8.

[11]Herbert P. Bix, *Hirohito and the Making of Modern Japan* (New York: HarperCollins, 2001), 676; John Dower, *Embracing Defeat* (New York: W. W. Norton & Company, 1999), 606.

[12]Ronald Takaki, *A Different Mirror: A History of Multicultural America* (New York: Back Bay Books, 2008), 156-58. This is also part of the history of Latinos in America, whose land in Texas and other territories were illegally invaded by Anglo settlers (cotton cultivators) who defied laws and restrictions of the Mexican government to build homes and possess lands. Eventually the American government sanctioned a war to overthrow the Mexican authorities and annex the land. Groups that are now minorities had a prior or rightful claim to land or political rule, but the earliest American settlers used force to overpower their resistance. Power is an inherent part of the history of the relationship between majority and minority cultures.

[13]Takaki, *A Different Mirror*, 84-89, 214-16.

[14]Takaki, *A Different Mirror*, 84.

[15]Geert Hofstede and Gert Jan Hofstede, *Cultures and Organizations: Software of the Mind: Intercultural Cooperation and Its Importance for Survival* (New York: McGraw-Hill Education, 2010).

[16]European Commission Against Racism and Intolerance, "Key Elements of National Legislation Against Racism and Racial Discrimination," December 13, 2002, www.coe.int/t/dghl/monitoring/ecri/activities/GPR/EN/Recommendation_N7/Recommendation_7_en.asp.

[17]Isabel Wilkerson, *The Warmth of Other Suns: The Epic Story of America's Great Migration* (New York: Vintage Books, 2010), 186-87.

[18]John M. Perkins, *Let Justice Roll Down* (Grand Rapids: Baker Books, 1976), 114.

[19]James H. Cone, *The Cross and the Lynching Tree* (Maryknoll, NY: Orbis Books, 2011), 4, 9.

[20]Kenneth B. Clark and Mamie P. Clark, "Racial Identification and Preference Among Negro Children," in *Readings in Social Psychology*, ed. Theodore M. Newcomb and Eugene L. Hartley (New York: Holt, Rinehart, and Winston, 1947), 169-78.

[21]You can take a test to determine your own biases at https://implicit.harvard .edu/implicit/takeatest.html.

[22]Examples of these advantages are from an article by Peggy McIntosh, "White Privilege: Unpacking the Invisible Knapsack," *Peace and Freedom Magazine*, July/August 1989, 10-12, as discussed in Beverly Daniel Tatum, *"Why Are All the Black Kids Sitting Together in the Cafeteria?" And Other Conversations About Race* (New York: Basic Books, 1997), 8.

[23]Andy Crouch, *Playing God: Redeeming the Gift of Power* (Downers Grove, IL: InterVarsity Press, 2013), 153-54.

[24]Soong-Chan Rah writes that "one of the most effective means of disengaging the church from the work of justice is making injustice a philosophical concept. With this high level of abstraction, it is easy to scapegoat individuals and move responsibility to the other rather than admit personal responsibility. When a mass shooting of children at a school occurs, we will claim that this horrible action is the result of just one crazed gunman rather than consider the possibility of a social-structure problem at work." Soong-Chan Rah, *Prophetic Lament: A Call for Justice in Troubled Times* (Downers Grove, IL: InterVarsity Press, 2015), 89.

[25]Hart, *Trouble I've Seen*, 53-55.

[26]Ken Wytsma, *The Myth of Equality: Uncovering the Roots of Injustice and Privilege* (Downers Grove, IL: InterVarsity Press, 2017), 25-26.

[27]Amanda Hess, "Asian American Actors Are Fighting for Visibility. They Will Not Be Ignored," May 25, 2016, www.nytimes.com/2016/05/29/movies/asian -american-actors-are-fighting-for-visibility-they-will-not-be-ignored.html.

[28]Steve Cofield, "Some Fans Take Issue with Velasquez's 'Brown Pride' Tattoo," Cagewriter, October 24, 2009, www.sports.yahoo.com/mma/blog/cagewriter /post/Some-fans-take-issue-with-Velasquez-s-Brown-Pri?urn=mma,197962.

[29]See Adam Guillen Jr., "Roy Nelson Contemplates 'White Pride' Tattoo, Thinks UFC Is Protecting Cain Velasquez," Yahoo! Sports, September 19,

2014, www.sports.yahoo.com/news/roy-nelson-contemplates-white
-pride-132456947.html, and "Is Cain Velasquez a Racist? He Has 'Brown
Pride' Tattooed on His Chest," Yahoo! Answers, www.answers.yahoo.com
/question/index?qid=20111121014837AAp7RIC.

[30]Sean Gregory, "All Across the Country, Athletes Are Fueling a Debate
About How America Defines Patriotism," October 3, 2016, www.time.com
/magazine/us/4503993/october-3rd-2016-vol-188-no-13-u-s.

[31]ESPN.com News Services, "Colin Kaepernick Joins Oakland High School
Football Team's Protest," ESPN, September 24, 2016, www.espn.com/nfl
/story/_/id/17624951/san-francisco-49ers-quarterback-colin-kaepernick
-joins-high-school-football-team-protest.

[32]Matt Vasilogambros, "Did Colin Kaepernick's Protest Fail?," *The Atlantic*,
August 30, 2016, www.theatlantic.com/news/archive/2016/08/colin
-kaepernick-protest-nfl/498065.

[33]Mark Sandritter, "A Timeline of Colin Kaepernick's National Anthem
Protest and the Athletes Who Joined Him," SBNation, November 6, 2016,
www.sbnation.com/2016/9/11/12869726/colin-kaepernick-national
-anthem-protest-seahawks-brandon-marshall-nfl.

[34]Michael Eric Dyson describes some helpful racial history behind the United
States flag, which was used as a weapon by a white man on a black lawyer
in Boston in 1976. Michael Eric Dyson, *Tears We Cannot Stop: A Sermon to
White America* (New York: St. Martin's Press, 2017), 113.

[35]Mark Bernardin, "Hollywood's Glaring Problem: White Actors Playing Asian
Characters," *Los Angeles Times*, April 18, 2016, www.latimes.com/entertainment
/movies/la-et-mn-racial-erasure-essay-20160418-story.html.

[36]Sterling HolyWhiteMountain, "The Great Failure of the Indians Mascot
Debate? Thinking of It Only as Racism," ESPN, October 26, 2016, www
.espn.com/mlb/story/_/id/17891581/great-failure-indians-mascot-debate
-thinking-only-racism.

[37]Daniel Hill clarifies that white supremacy is a system of ideology that must
be dismantled, and it is not the same as the personhood of white individuals,
who are made in the image of God and are therefore inherently worthy and
valuable. Daniel Hill, *White Awake: An Honest Look at What It Means to Be
White* (Downers Grove, IL: InterVarsity Press, 2017), 147.

[38]In 2018, Cleveland Indians CEO Paul Dolan, under pressure from Major
League Baseball commissioner Rob Manfred, decided that the team would

stop using the Chief Wahoo logo on their uniforms in 2019 and gradually phase out general use in the years to come. As one might imagine, this decision has been polarizing. David Waldstein, "Cleveland Indians Will Abandon Chief Wahoo Logo Next Year," *New York Times*, January 29, 2018, www.nytimes.com/2018/01/29/sports/baseball/cleveland-indians-chief-wahoo-logo.html.

[39]Takaki, *A Different Mirror*, 4-5.

[40]Ronald Takaki, *Strangers from a Different Shore: A History of Asian Americans* (New York: Back Bay Books, 1998), xv.

[41]Jeff Chang, *Who We Be: A Cultural History of Race in Post–Civil Rights America* (New York: St. Martin's Press, 2014), 116.

[42]In this case, the incident was the shootings in Ferguson. Wallis, *America's Original Sin*, 18.

[43]Carol Anderson, *White Rage: The Unspoken Truth of Our Racial Divide* (New York: Bloomsbury, 2016), 19.

[44]Michelle Alexander, *The New Jim Crow: Mass Incarceration in the Age of Colorblindness* (New York: The New Press, 2012), 21-22.

[45]Michael Omi and Howard Winant, *Racial Formation in the United States: From the 1960s to the 1990s* (New York: Routledge, 1994), 118-19. This cycle of "race and reaction" is not new. According to Omi and Winant and D. W. Griffith's *Birth of a Nation*, the resurfacing of whites who feel dislocated by social changes and feel critical of authorities who are too "weak, naive, and corrupt to maintain America's 'true' identity" has existed since the Civil War.

[46]Omi and Winant, *Racial Formation in the United States*, 117-20.

[47]Roxanne Dunbar-Ortiz, *An Indigenous Peoples' History of the United States* (Boston: Beacon Press, 2014), 229, 235.

3 DOMESTICATION

[1]Michael Luo, "'Go Back to China': Readers Respond to Racist Insults Shouted at a New York Times Editor," *New York Times*, October 10, 2016, www.nytimes.com/2016/10/11/nyregion/go-back-to-china-readers-respond-to-racist-insults-shouted-at-a-new-york-times-editor.html?.

[2]Hope King, "#Thisis2016 Rallies Asian Americans Against Racist Encounters," CNN, October 10, 2016, money.cnn.com/2016/10/10/technology/thisis2016-michael-luo-nytimes/index.html.

[3]Michael Luo, "An Open Letter to the Woman Who Told My Family to Go Back to China," *New York Times*, October 9, 2016, www.nytimes .com/2016/10/10/nyregion/to-the-woman-who-told-my-family-to-go -back-to-china.html?.

[4]Walter Littlemoon, *They Called Me Uncivilized: The Memoir of an Everyday Lakota Man from Wounded Knee* (Bloomington, IN: iUniverse, 2009), 42-47.

[5]Littlemoon, *They Called Me Uncivilized*, 12; Takaki, *A Different Mirror*, 217-18. This effort to "domesticate" Native Americans happened not only through boarding schools, but through the simple act of moving Native tribes from the free plains and lands they owned to other places in the West or allocated plots of lands (reservations). Even General Custer, who himself killed many Native Americans, articulated their plight: "To civilize Indians would be to require them to abandon their way of life as warriors, and to sacrifice their manhood by working for a living. Custer thought that 'if' he were an Indian, he would choose the 'free open plains' rather than submit to the 'confined limits of a reservation.' Death would be preferable to life in a cage."

[6]Littlemoon, *They Called Me Uncivilized*, 52-59.

[7]Littlemoon, *They Called Me Uncivilized*, 58-59.

[8]Littlemoon, *They Called Me Uncivilized*, 59.

[9]Randy Woodley, *Living in Color: Embracing God's Passion for Ethnic Diversity* (Downers Grove, IL: InterVarsity Press, 2001), 111.

[10]Jeanne Wakatsuki Houston and James D. Houston, *Farewell to Manzanar: A True Story of Japanese American Experience During and After the World War II Internment* (New York: Random House, 1973), 127.

[11]This sentiment that Houston "deserved it" is much like the self-blame and internalization covered in chapter 1.

[12]Houston and Houston, *Farewell to Manzanar*, 130.

[13]I remember one of my minority friends telling me that he thought dating a white woman was the ultimate sign of having "succeeded" in earning a status of respect.

[14]Houston and Houston, *Farewell to Manzanar*, 109, 172.

[15]Elizabeth Cohen, "Push to Achieve Tied to Suicide in Asian-American Women," CNN, May 16, 2007, www.cnn.com/2007/HEALTH/05/16 /asian.suicides.

[16]Kyung Lah, "Plastic Surgery Boom as Asians Seek 'Western' Look," CNN, May 23, 2011, www.cnn.com/2011/WORLD/asiapcf/05/19/korea.beauty /index.html.

[17]Leah Gunning Francis, *Ferguson & Faith: Sparking Leadership & Awakening Community* (Danvers, MA: Chalice Press, 2015), 70, 88.

[18]Marissa Payne, "Lou Holtz on Immigrant 'Invasion': 'I Don't Want to Become You,'" *Washington Post*, July 19, 2016, www.washingtonpost.com /news/early-lead/wp/2016/07/19/lou-holtz-on-immigrant-invasion -i-dont-want-to-become-you.

[19]Beverly Daniel Tatum, *"Why Are All the Black Kids Sitting Together in the Cafeteria?" And Other Conversations About Race* (New York: Basic Books, 1997), 5.

[20]As first defined in David T. Wellman, *Portraits of White Racism* (Cambridge: Cambridge University Press, 1993).

[21]Tatum, *"Why Are All the Black Kids Sitting Together in the Cafeteria?,"* 7, 10.

[22]For instance, as far back at the 1800s, American magazines depicted Chinese men as savage vampires with slanted eyes. Laws were put into place to prohibit marriage between Chinese men and White women. There were even ideas to put Asian immigrants onto reservations. Takaki, *Strangers from a Different Shore*, 101-2.

[23]Arnav Adhikari, "The National Book Awards Make a Powerful Statement," *The Atlantic*, November 17, 2016, www.theatlantic.com/entertainment /archive/2016/11/the-national-book-awards-colson-whitehead-john-lewis -ibram-kendi/508064. Research has even shown that systemic injustice can be measured in the impact of stress and discrimination on infant mortality rates in the African American community. Zoe Carpenter, "What's Killing America's Black Infants?," *The Nation*, February 15, 2017, www.thenation .com/article/whats-killing-americas-black-infants.

[24]Tatum, *"Why Are All the Black Kids Sitting Together in the Cafeteria?,"* 11.

[25]InterVarsity Christian Fellowship, "Approaching Differences Diagram," https://2100.intervarsity.org/resources/approaching-differences-diagram.

[26]Study.com, "Cultural Adaptation: Definition, Theory, Stages & Examples," https://study.com/academy/lesson/cultural-adaptation-definition-theory -stages-examples.html.

[27]Bhikhu Parekh, "Unity and Diversity in Multicultural Societies" (International Institute for Labour Studies: Geneva, March 2005), 5.

[28]Harry Kitano and Roger Daniels, *Asian Americans: Emerging Minorities*, 2nd ed. (Englewood Cliffs, NJ: Prentice-Hall, 1995).

[29]In fact, over the years we have come to see that when minorities speak their hearts and minds, it can be a sign of success that they feel safe enough to do so. Just because people are expressing anger and pain doesn't mean things are not well. On the contrary, it's often the natural outpouring that happens after decades of keeping feelings and thoughts within ourselves, when the "dam" of silence and silencing is finally broken.

[30]Ta-Nehisi Coates, *Between the World and Me* (New York: Spiegel & Grau, 2015), 96-97, 151.

4 WEARINESS

[1]Some of the dynamics of power and voice related to groups and gatherings are covered in Adam S. McHugh's *Introverts in the Church* (Downers Grove, IL: InterVarsity Press, 2017) and Eric Law's *The Wolf Shall Dwell with the Lamb* (Atlanta: Chalice Press, 1993).

[2]Of course, the reason behind any exodus, as Helen Lee identified in her article on Asian churches, is that deepest needs are not being met. Helen Lee, "Silent Exodus: Can the East Asian Church in America Reverse the Flight of Its Next Generation?," *Christianity Today*, August 12, 1996, www .christianitytoday.com/ct/1996/august12/6t9050.html.

[3]Brian Virtue, "Why Ethnic Minority Leaders Leave Ministry Organizations," December 11, 2012, www.brianvirtue.org/2012/12/whyethnic minoritystaffleaveorgs.

[4]Something like this did happen. In the 1970s, Stan Inouye started Cru's first-ever Intercultural Ministries program to facilitate learning about Asian American, Latino, African American, and Native American cultures and how they impact ministry. The program only lasted about a year before it was discontinued—I've talked to many minority staff who believe this is because the group wasn't yielding enough numerical ministry "results."

[5]There are some great resources on ministry burnout that have been created over the years. For instance, InterVarsity Press resources *Doing Good Without Giving Up* by Ben Lowe, *The World Is Not Ours to Save* by Tyler Wigg-Stevenson, and *Fail* by J. R. Briggs. Some IVP resources for soul care include *Strengthening the Soul of Your Leadership* by Ruth Haley Barton,

The Vulnerable Pastor by Mandy Smith, *Preventing Ministry Failure* by Michael Todd Wilson and Brad Hoffman, or *Resilient Ministry* by Bob Burns, Donald Guthrie, and Tasha Chapman.

[6]Amy Adkins, "What Millennials Want from Work and Life," Gallup News, May 11, 2016, http://news.gallup.com/businessjournal/191435/millennials -work-life.aspx. See also "How Millennials Want to Work and Live," Gallup News, http://news.gallup.com/reports/189830/millennials-work-live.aspx.

[7]Isabel Wilkerson, *The Warmth of Other Suns: The Epic Story of America's Great Migration* (New York: Vintage Books, 2010), 42. The context of these years included post–Reconstruction realities, including economic struggles, the withdrawal of northern troops, and the institution of Jim Crow laws.

[8]Wilkerson, *Warmth of Other Suns*, 83-84.

[9]"Fred Korematsu: Abbreviated Biography," Fred T. Korematsu Institute, www.korematsuinstitute.org/fred-t-korematsu-lifetime.

[10]Steven A. Chin, *When Justice Failed: The Fred Korematsu Story* (New York: Steck-Vaughn Company, 1993), 61.

[11]"Looking Back at Japanese Internment Camps," NPR, December 5, 2007, www.npr.org/templates/story/story.php?storyId=16919643.

[12]Duncan Tonatiuh, *Separate Is Never Equal: Sylvia Mendez and Her Family's Fight for Desegregation* (New York: Abrams Books, 2014), 17.

[13]Tonatiuh, *Separate Is Never Equal*, 33.

[14]Mark Charles, "Remarks Shared by Mark Charles at #ApacheStronghold Rally on Capitol Hill in Washington DC," July 22, 2015, http:// wirelesshogan.blogspot.com/2015/07/remarks-shared-by-mark-charles-at -apachestronghold-dc.html.

[15]David Park, "An Open Letter from the Asian American Community to the Evangelical Church," October 13, 2013, http://nextgenerasianchurch .com/2013/10/13/an-open-letter-to-the-evangelical-church-from-the -asian-american-community.

[16]Edgar H. Schein, *Organizational Culture and Leadership*, 5th ed. (Hoboken, NY: John Wiley & Sons, 2017), 8.

[17]Also, the forces of racial reactivity will likely resist organizational changes related to diversity. Well-intentioned white organizational leaders may face pressure from financial donors to reverse or slow these changes.

[18]Schein, *Organizational Culture and Leadership*, 338-39, 353.

● 5 CHALLENGES IN ORGANIZATIONAL DEVELOPMENT

[1]Soong-Chan Rah, *Prophetic Lament: A Call for Justice in Troubled Times* (Downers Grove, IL: InterVarsity Press, 2015), 58. Also in Soong-Chan Rah, *Many Colors: Cultural Intelligence for a Changing Church* (Chicago: Moody Publishers, 2010), 44.

[2]Michael O. Emerson and Christian Smith, *Divided By Faith: Evangelical Religion and the Problem of Race in America* (New York: Oxford University Press, 2000), 70, 75.

[3]Patrick Lencioni, *The Advantage: Why Organizational Health Trumps Everything Else in Business* (San Francisco: Jossey-Bass, 2012), 190.

[4]Edgar H. Schein, *Organizational Culture and Leadership*, 5th ed. (Hoboken, NJ: John Wiley & Sons, 2017), 354.

[5]Brenda Salter McNeil, *Roadmap to Reconciliation: Moving Communities into Unity, Wholeness and Justice* (Downers Grove, IL: InterVarsity Press, 2016), 69.

[6]Lencioni, *The Advantage*, 23.

[7]If you have a large organization and are needing to demonstrate that you're drawing from a larger pool of leaders, you can design a couple larger initial "input" meetings first. You can break people into smaller groups (e.g., three people per group) to work on specific pieces of input. After these initial meetings, you can launch the change agent team to follow through on the input.

[8]Schein, *Organizational Culture and Leadership*, 155, 204.

[9]Schein, *Organizational Culture and Leadership*, 18.

[10]McNeil, *Roadmap to Reconciliation*, 46.

[11]McNeil, *Roadmap to Reconciliation*, 42.

[12]Schein, *Organizational Culture and Leadership*, 233-51.

[13]Or an organization's survival anxiety must be higher than learning anxiety; there must be a greater crisis or consequence of *not* changing, than of changing. Schein, *Organizational Culture and Leadership*, 328.

[14]Schein, *Organizational Culture and Leadership*, 147.

[15]Emerson and Smith, *Divided by Faith*, 171.

[16]Lencioni, *The Advantage*, 3.

[17]I intentionally chose to use an international example here, to explore which dynamics of power and diversity might be similar outside of the United States.

[18]Cru has a Strategic Leadership Initiative (SLI) cohort that they are seeking to diversify, and which I was invited to join.

[19]Kate Shellnutt, "InterVarsity Names a Historic New President," *Christianity Today*, May 16, 2016, www.christianitytoday.com/ct/2016/may-web-only /intervarsity-names-historic-new-president.html.

[20]Lencioni, *The Advantage*, 15.

[21]Lencioni, *The Advantage*, 142.

[22]McNeil, *Roadmap to Reconciliation*, 83, 88.

[23]Lencioni, *The Advantage*, 15-16.

⬤ 6 SEEING PAIN WITH EYES OF COMPASSION

[1]Robert H. Fuson, ed., *The Log of Christopher Columbus* (New York: Philomel Books, 1992).

[2]Roxanne Dunbar-Ortiz, *An Indigenous Peoples' History of the United States* (Boston: Beacon Press, 2014), 3.

[3]Dunbar-Ortiz, *An Indigenous Peoples' History*, 64-65.

[4]Sarah Shin, *Beyond Colorblind: Redeeming Our Ethnic Journey* (Downers Grove, IL: InterVarsity Press, 2017), 8.

[5]Rev. Martin Luther King Jr., "The Other America," Grosse Pointe High School, March 14, 1968, www.gphistorical.org/mlk/mlkspeech.

[6]Carolyn Custis James, *The Gospel of Ruth: Loving God Enough to Break the Rules* (Grand Rapids: Zondervan, 2008), 42.

[7]James, *Gospel of Ruth*, 116.

[8]Bryan Stevenson, *Just Mercy: A Story of Justice and Redemption* (New York: Spiegel & Grau, 2014), 290.

[9]Grace Ji-Sun Kim, *Embracing the Other: The Transformative Spirit of Love* (Grand Rapids: Eerdmans, 2015), 56.

[10]James H. Cone, *The Cross and the Lynching Tree* (Maryknoll, NY: Orbis Books, 2011), 66.

[11]See #Linsanity on Next Generasian Church: http://nextgenerasianchurch .com/tag/linsanity.

[12]Christopher Hunt, "Lin Makes Lakers Believe the Hype," ESPN, February 11, 2012, www.espn.com/blog/new-york/knicks/post/_/id/11352/lin-makes -lakers-believe-the-hype.

[13]Many NBA analysts marveled at how Lin had been so invisible given his high skill level. Tim Legler said, "I've never seen it happen. . . . A guy that had three different teams look at him and not see what we're seeing now?"

Jesse Washington, "Asian-Americans Rejoice as Lin Smashes Stereotypes," Fox News, February 17, 2012, foxnews.com/sports/2012/02/17/asian -americans-rejoice-as-lin-smashes-stereotypes.html. Former NBA commissioner David Stern claimed that Lin's ethnicity as Asian American could have contributed to this. David Barron, "Lin Tells '60 Minutes' His Ethnicity Played a Role in Him Going Undrafted," *Houston Chronicle*, April 5, 2013, blog.chron.com/sportsupdate/2013/04/lin-tells-60-minutes-his-ethnicity -may-have-stymied-college-recruiting-offers.

[14]Washington, "Asian-Americans Rejoice as Lin Smashes Stereotypes." Timothy Dalrymple also describes the significance of Jeremy Lin to Asian American leaders in his book *Jeremy Lin: The Reason for the Linsanity* (New York: Center Street, 2012).

[15]J. J. Redick, "Jeremy Lin Joins the Vertical Podcast," *The Chronicles of Redick*, July 25, 2016, www.stitcher.com/podcast/art19/the-vertical-podcast-with -jj-redick/e/45512954.

[16]Ohm Youngmisuk, "Jeremy Lin Says Racist Remarks He Heard from Opponents Were Worse in NCAA Than NBA," ESPN, May 11, 2017, www .espn.com/nba/story/_/id/19353394/jeremy-lin-brooklyn-nets-says-heard -racist-remarks-more-frequently-college-nba.

[17]Jeremy Lin, "So . . . About My Hair," *The Players' Tribune*, October 3, 2017, www.theplayerstribune.com/jeremy-lin-brooklyn-nets-about-my-hair.

[18]Indeed, millions of Latinos flooded the streets in May 2006 in protest of US immigration reforms.

[19]And originally the property of Native Americans.

[20]Ronald Takaki, *A Different Mirror: A History of Multicultural America* (New York: Back Bay Books, 2008), 165.

[21]Juan Gonzalez, *Harvest of Empire: A History of Latinos in America* (New York: Penguin Group, 2011), 76-77.

[22]This has happened many times throughout United States history. Between the 1880s and 1930s, millions of Mexicans were recruited to work on the railroads in the southwestern and midwestern states. When the Great Depression hit and jobs became scarce, an estimated one million Mexican workers were forcibly deported south of the border.

[23]Jim Wallis, *America's Original Sin: Racism, White Privilege, and the Bridge to a New America* (Grand Rapids: Brazos Press, 2016), 167.

[24]From his novel *Invisible Man*. Clint Smith, "Ralph Ellison's 'Invisible Man' as a Parable of Our Time," *New Yorker*, December 4, 2016, www.newyorker .com/books/page-turner/ralph-ellisons-invisible-man-as-a-parable-of-our -time. *Invisible Man* is incidentally being developed into a television series. See Daniel Holloway, "Ralph Ellison's 'Invisible Man' Series Adaptation in the Works at Hulu," *Variety*, October 26, 2017, https://variety.com/2017/tv /news/invisible-man-hulu-series-1202599486.

7 STEWARDING POWER WITH HANDS OF ADVOCACY

[1]Young Lee Hertig and Chloe Sun, eds., *Mirrored Reflections: Reframing Biblical Characters* (Eugene, OR: Wipf & Stock, 2010), 101.

[2]Daniel R. Sanchez, *Hispanic Realities Impacting America: Implications for Evangelism and Missions* (Fort Worth, TX: Church Starting Network, 2006), 108.

[3]Christena Cleveland, *Disunity in Christ: Uncovering the Hidden Forces That Keep Us Apart* (Downers Grove, IL: InterVarsity Press, 2013), 123.

[4]Peter Cha, S. Steve Kang, and Helen Lee, eds., *Growing Healthy Asian American Churches: Ministry Insights from Groundbreaking Congregations* (Downers Grove, IL: InterVarsity Press, 2006), 147.

[5]Cha, Kang, and Lee, *Growing Healthy Asian American Churches*, 65-66.

[6]Jon Huckins and Jer Swigart, *Mending the Divides: Creative Love in a Conflicted World* (Downers Grove, IL: InterVarsity Press, 2017), 104-5.

[7]Kyung Lah, "The LA Riots Were a Rude Awakening for Korean-Americans," CNN, April 29, 2017, www.cnn.com/2017/04/28/us/la-riots-korean -americans/index.html.

[8]Karen Grigsby Bates, "How Koreatown Rose from the Ashes of L.A. Riots," NPR, April 27, 2012, www.npr.org/2012/04/27/151524921/how -koreatown-rose-from-the-ashes-of-l-a-riots.

[9]Some in both of these minority communities believe that whites turned blacks and Koreans on each other, as the police abandoned the area of violence to leave them to fight: "Robert Lee Ahn . . . watched the unfolding chaos on television, wondering why the police would leave his father alone as Koreatown burned. . . . 'The community felt abandoned by law enforcement,' said Ahn, adding that [his father's real estate business] tenants managed to protect the strip mall from being set on fire. 'They were deemed

expendable. The reason was simple: a lack of political voice and political power.'" Lah, "The LA Riots Were a Rude Awakening for Korean-Americans."

[10]Many centuries earlier, the prophet Isaiah had predicted that the Messiah would model such behavior: "He was treated badly, but he never protested. He said nothing, like a lamb being led away to be killed" (Isaiah 53:7).

[11]James H. Cone, *The Cross and the Lynching Tree* (Maryknoll, NY: Orbis Books, 2011), 21-22.

[12]Sarah Parvini and Victoria Kim, "25 Years After Racial Tensions Erupted, Black and Korean Communities Reflect on L.A. Riots," *Los Angeles Times*, April 29, 2017, www.latimes.com/local/lanow/la-me-ln-la-riots-unity -meeting-20170429-story.html.

[13]Rachel Glickhouse and Jessica Weiss, "For Some Latinos and Asian-Americans, Black Lives Do Matter," Univision News, July 8, 2016, www .univision.com/univision-news/united-states/for-some-latinos-and-asian -americans-black-lives-do-matter.

[14]Letters for Black Lives: An Open Letter Project on Anti-Blackness, "Dear Mom, Dad, Uncle, Auntie: Black Lives Matter to Us, Too," July 11, 2016, https://lettersforblacklives.com/dear-mom-dad-uncle-auntie-black-lives -matter-to-us-too-7ca577d59f4c.

[15]Glickhouse and Weiss, "For Some Latinos and Asian-Americans, Black Lives Do Matter."

[16]A historical example is of when Japanese American and Mexican American workers formed a labor association and successful strike in Oxnard in 1903. Shortly after, the American Federation of Labor sought to split the two minority groups, offering to charter the association under the condition that Japanese and Chinese workers would not be granted membership. However, Mexican leader J. M. Lizarras refused the offer since it did not recognize other minorities. This is an example of a minority group who was given a tempting offer to marginalize another community, but chose to reject the philosophy of "limited good" and shared their platform and voice with other minorities. Ronald Takaki, *A Different Mirror: A History of Multicultural America* (New York: Back Bay Books, 2008), 175.

[17]Tara John, "5 Ways Prince Harry and Meghan Markle's Engagement Is Groundbreaking," *Time*, November 27, 2017, http://time.com/5037634 /meghan-markle-engagement-prince-harry-groundbreaking.

[18]Meghan Markle, "I'm More Than an 'Other,'" *Elle*, December 22, 2016, www.elleuk.com/life-and-culture/news/a26855/more-than-an-other.

[19]Cha, Kang, and Lee, *Growing Healthy Asian American Churches*, 162.

[20]While other minority cohorts have applied similar principles, the Daniel Project has been more successful for some communities than others, and InterVarsity continues to work on supporting women of color to navigate organizational structures.

[21]Walter Littlemoon, *They Called Me Uncivilized: The Memoir of an Everyday Lakota Man from Wounded Knee* (Bloomington, IN: iUniverse, 2009), 80-89.

8 REFRAMING THE PAST WITH A HEART OF WISDOM

[1]Eli Saslow, "The White Flight of Derek Black," *Washington Post*, October 15, 2016, www.washingtonpost.com/national/the-white-flight-of-derek -black/2016/10/15/ed5f906a-8f3b-11e6-a6a3-d50061aa9fae_story.html? See "Finalist: Eli Saslow of *The Washington Post*" at www.pulitzer.org/finalists /eli-saslow-1.

[2]In 1982, a Chinese American man named Vincent Chin was brutally beaten and murdered outside a Detroit restaurant by Ronald Ebens and Michael Nitz, two white auto workers. According to eyewitnesses, they had gotten into an argument with Chin and expressed how upset they were that people who looked like Chin were taking away their jobs. There had recently been many layoffs at the nearby auto plants due to an increasing market share of Japanese automakers and Chrysler's sales of captively imported Mitsubishi models. Of course, Chin wasn't Japanese, but to Ebens and Nitz it didn't matter. Their anger wasn't about Chin himself, as they barely knew the young man. What drove them to an act of crosscultural violence was their deep fears—feeling threatened at their core. Chin was the scapegoat. One could argue that racism at its heart is about scapegoating. Ebens and Nitz were sentenced to manslaughter, which was later overturned on their appeal. This caused an uproar in the Asian American community, which rallied to create public pressure for federal prosecution. See Ronald Takaki, *Strangers from a Different Shore: A History of Asian Americans* (New York: Back Bay Books, 1998), 481-84.

[3]Ronald Takaki, *A Different Mirror: A History of Multicultural America* (New York: Back Bay Books, 2008), 189-90.

⁴Juan Gonzalez, *Harvest of Empire: A History of Latinos in America* (New York: Penguin Group, 2011), 100-103.

⁵Takaki, *Strangers from a Different Shore*, 297.

⁶Takaki, *Strangers from a Different Shore*, 326-27.

⁷Takaki, *Strangers from a Different Shore*, 454.

⁸Michael Omi and Howard Winant, *Racial Formation in the United States: From the 1960s to the 1990s* (New York: Routledge, 1994), 116.

⁹Takaki, *A Different Mirror*, 60.

¹⁰Adrian Pei, Jennifer Pei, Destino Kristy, Donnie Begay, and Renee Begay, "Six Postures of Ethnic Minority Culture Towards Majority Culture," July 2012, www.cru.org/content/dam/cru/legacy/2012/07/Six-Postures.pdf.

¹¹Brian Virtue, Destino Eric, and Tommy Forester, "Five Majority Culture Postures Toward Ethnic Minority Ministry," www.cru.org/content/dam/cru/legacy/2012/07/Five-Majority-Culture.pdf.

¹²Michael O. Emerson and Christian Smith, *Divided by Faith: Evangelical Religion and the Problem of Race in America* (New York: Oxford University Press, 2000), 113.

¹³Daniel Hill, *White Awake: An Honest Look at What It Means to Be White* (Downers Grove, IL: InterVarsity Press, 2017), 72.

¹⁴Hill, *White Awake*, 90.

¹⁵Sarah Shin, *Beyond Colorblind: Redeeming Our Ethnic Journey* (Downers Grove, IL: InterVarsity Press, 2017), 82.

¹⁶Some prefer to use the term *conciliation* since they believe there was never an ideal state of peace back to which we can all be reconciled.

¹⁷Brenda Salter McNeil, *Roadmap to Reconciliation: Moving Communities into Unity, Wholeness and Justice* (Downers Grove, IL: InterVarsity Press, 2016), 22.

¹⁸Linda Lee, *The Bruce Lee Story* (Santa Clarita, CA: Ohara Publications, Inc., 1989), 52.

¹⁹Justin Worland, "What to Know About the Dakota Access Pipeline Protests," *Time*, October 28, 2016, http://time.com/4548566/dakota-access-pipeline-standing-rock-sioux.

²⁰Randy Woodley, *Living in Color: Embracing God's Passion for Ethnic Diversity* (Downers Grove, IL: InterVarsity Press, 2001), 186-88. Also see Montana Department of Transportation, "US 93—Wildlife Crossing Structures in Use," www.mdt.mt.gov/pubinvolve/us93info/wildlife_crossings.shtml.

²¹Woodley, *Living in Color*, 47.

[22]In Rev. Paul Sorrentino's *A Transforming Vision*, his African American friend writes, "I'm sure I could construct practical strategies for building mentoring relationships across cultures, but no strategy or tactic can work without genuine compassion, humility and love from the mentor in the relationship. This is especially true if the mentor is from a race that has historically held power. It is imperative that mentors of the majority culture enter interracial mentor relationships with a servant's attitude and genuine love and compassion." Paul Sorrentino, *A Transforming Vision: Multiethnic Fellowship in College and in the Church* (South Hadley, MA: Doorlight Publications, 2011), 78.

[23]Saslow, "The White Flight of Derek Black."

[24]On an August 2017 NPR interview, black musician Daryl Davis shared about how for the past thirty years, he has befriended members of the Ku Klux Klan. Through friendship, talking, and bonding through a common love of music, Davis shares that two hundred Klansmen have given up their robes. He claims that some of them admitted they had never sat down and talked to a black man before. Dwane Brown, "How One Man Convinced 200 Ku Klux Klan Members to Give Up Their Robes," NPR, August 20, 2017, www.npr.org/2017/08/20/544861933/how-one-man-convinced-200 -ku-klux-klan-members-to-give-up-their-robes.

9 THE CHALLENGE AND THE OPPORTUNITY

[1]Kannan Srikanth, Sarah Harvey, and Randall Peterson, "A Dynamic Perspective on Diverse Teams: Moving from the Dual-Process Model to a Dynamic Coordination-Based Model of Diverse Team Performance," January 27, 2016, www.tandfonline.com/doi/full/10.1080/19416520.2016 .1120973.

NAME AND SUBJECT INDEX

SCRIPTURE INDEX

ABOUT THE AUTHOR

Adrian Pei is an organizational development consultant and leadership trainer who works for two of the largest corporate and ministry organizations in the world. He has specialized in speaking and writing about race and diversity for over a decade as part of Epic Movement, the Asian American ministry of Cru, where he also served as associate national director of leadership development. He has earned degrees at Stanford University and Fuller Theological Seminary, but his education continues every day of his life.

Adrian is not related to I. M. Pei, but he is related to one of his heroes, Bruce Lee. His name in Chinese means "honest scholar," and he tries to live up to it. In his free time, he enjoys studying song lyrics, blogging, hitting tennis balls, cooking new recipes, and playing strategy board games. He and his family live in southern California.

Twitter: @adrianpei
adrianpei.com
minoritybook.com